The Real Proof of Heaven:
What & Where Is It?

The Real Proof of Heaven:
What & Where Is It?

Sam Oputa

Sam Oputa, Copyright © 2021

ALL RIGHTS RESERVED

The author is hereby established as the sole holder of the copyright.

ISBN-13: 9788500465436

Those who can make you believe absurdities can make you commit atrocities…Voltaire 1765.

Oh, by the way, if you believe in Heaven, this book helps you prove it because Heaven is real. Is Heaven as real as you've been taught to believe? See Heaven in all its glory. Read about God sitting on His Throne.

Contents

About the Author iv

Preface viii

Chapter One   Heaven, the Perception....1

Chapter Two   Perception of Heaven by Other Societies 10

Chapter Three   Religion as a Groupthink? 22

Chapter Four   Is There a Heaven?.........31

Chapter Five   Heaven as another Dimension?...44

Chapter Six   Gathered With His Fathers ..62

Chapter Seven   Other Dimensions?........67

Chapter Eight   In My Father's House......78

Chapter Nine   Is There a Heaven—the Reality..84

Chapter Ten   Conclusion: Proof of Heaven 105

Bibliography 136

About the Author

Raised in an environment where religion was never forced, Sam Oputa became a Protestant, then later a practicing Catholic. He attended Baruch College of the City University of New York.

Sam Oputa is also the author of God Is Not Enough, Messiah Needed, Faith or Reason, Immaterial Existence, No Map to Reality, All the God We Cannot See and Why Was Man Created?

Psalm 78:23-24

*Though he had commanded the clouds from above, and <u>opened the doors of heaven,</u>
And had rained down manna upon them to eat, and had given them of the corn of heaven.*

Heaven has doors? You will see the relevance of this question after reading *The Real Proof of Heaven: What & Where Is It*.

Preface

In a world where disinformation and misinformation run rampant, truth has become more difficult to pin down to one definition. Truth, therefore, becomes relative.
There are now alternative truths. Often, the "truth" all these years was a lie. It is sad. It is disheartening. Sometimes, you may wonder how easy even intelligent people get fooled into taking such disinformation as truths. It is shameful. Are you not even tempted to audit our education systems? Who set up the education systems? Of course, they are not the common street-smart people we associate with all the days of our lives.

Today, it is a fad to flood the airwaves and printing presses around the world with firehoses of falsehoods and people are listening and believing the lies as truth. Those who are benefitting financially from the lies are succeeding and greatly too. Do you ever wonder why people believe in so much crazy theories these days? It is as if people are so confused, they are getting more stupid by the minute.

There are so many falsehoods out there. Such falsehoods have permeated our social, economic, and especially our religious lives so much so that it seems we are rewarding the fabricators of big lies by getting glued to and carried away by the alternate truths.

It feels, sometimes, like we are purging the reality-based people and rewarding and elevating the clearest and loudest voices that promote alternate truth.
How we all got bamboozled is left to speculation, misinterpretations, and outright fabrications. But they are chipping away at the fabric of our societies with their lies.

That there are millions of people worldwide who were willing to overthrow the truth of 2+2=4 in order to keep alternate truths in power, who would follow these dark lies rather than acknowledge unwelcome truths—the real truths—is perhaps due to economic and political enticements they set themselves up to reap thereafter. Some of us fail to realize that life is never forever. Perhaps, until we start to think about humanity and individual legacies, the big lies will be growing by leaps and bounds.

Thus, the level of complicity by those engaging in these alternate truths is a greed that they wish to justify by the claim "If you can't beat them, you join them" refrain. The intent is to articulate and so justify a lie as a different point of view. They are the loudest in promoting a place called Heaven. Ask yourself: why do they do this? It is an attempt to control. Firstly, they feed you ignorance and then when you fall for it, they pounce and control you with same ignorance. Either way, it will be the same lose-lose situation for the listener but a win-win situation for the influencer. They know that the juice is worth the squeeze. So, they will keep at it.

Standing on the outside looking in, some might not know it is all a big lie. Some people who can perceive these alternate truths have expressed frustration with alternate truth peddlers.

The peddlers who seem to be "believing the garbage that they are being fed 24/7 on the internet, airwaves, and religious places, take pride in amplifying what they themselves know is a big lie.

What should they care? After all, there are men of the cloth that travel only by privately owned jets that can fly nonstop from one continent to another. The big lies are paying off, big time.

In the final analysis, the big lies have become our big problem that must be solved. The way forward and the question is: How are we going to really almost deprogram these people who have signed up for the *big lie cult* that pervades the religious, social, cultural, political, and economic spheres of our lives? Big lies were here yesterday; Big lies are here today and would be here tomorrow. To the peddlers of big lies, the lies are like sunshine on a cloudy day.

In almost all situations, makers of the "big lie" know they almost always need a villain. They need someone to blame. In this scenario, like most other scenarios, they need someone, something, or a group different from theirs whom they could get others to hate.

As is the case in most religions, the scenarios are always a story of good versus evil. Made up big lie—the type that would incite an angry mob, only works if the person seeking power or money, provides the audience with someone who personifies evil. Be warned! What you are about to read in this title is going to be heartrending for many. But then, for one—anybody—who has been living a lie since birth, finding the truth should be distressing. However, the truth though upsetting and distressing when found, can also set you free and make you whole.

If there is no true villain, that is not a problem at all. All they need do is to invent one. So, like the stories in the Bible, storytellers/interpreters decided to make Satan the villain in their story just as hell is made a villainous place in the same story. Almost always, defendants will decide who or what to make as the villain in the story.

In these big lies, they make the earth to be "flat" and tell you that 2 plus 2 is anything but four. In reality, we know that the earth is round and that 2 plus 2 can only be four. These are not assumptions but basic facts. Facts are facts. No ifs and buts. Facts are not beliefs by faith or make-believe or "I believe this and disbelieve that."

The framers of these big lies are in the business of giving legs and hands to the big lies so that the lies can travel far and wide. If you then come across individuals whose belief systems were borrowed from the big lies, you must not make assumptions that they are idiots. They have only imbibed one or more of the big lies. A step by step logical explanation with logical truths may bring them away from earlier imbibed beliefs.

They have bought into misinformation and, perhaps, misinterpretations. The big lies seem to be as a result of misinterpretation of literary works, conspiracy theories, and or simply that the truth is hardly and rarely the best and stimulatingly tantalizing story. Sometimes, it takes a lot to convince believers that there is no such thing as divine, unless, divine is an allegory yet to be decoded.

As Wikipedia nicely puts it "Conspiracy theories usually deny consensus or cannot be proven using the historical or scientific method and are not to be confused with research concerning verified conspiracies such as …" The bottom line is for you and I and indeed for everyone to control their narratives. Every life is a story.

You either tell your story the way you want it or you let others tell your story for you. When others tell your story, you have conceded your narrative to others. When you listen to big lies, you are letting others write your narrative and, therefore, confining and controlling your life.

Every big lie and those who manufacture the lie do so for a reason. They do it to gain power or money. They do it for control. It is a narcissistic behavior. One of the most important tools available to a narcissist is the ability to control the narrative.

Some of these narrators are making big bucks selling lies. Sometimes, the faces you see as the narrators are not the powers behind the microphone. They just read the prepared narratives and get paid. They have sold their earthly purposes for the proverbial bowl of porridge. It is all about manipulation for power and money.

Look around you and pinpoint those you listen to. How do they control the narrative? Think of a lawyer, a friend, a pastor, a governor, a president etc. Do they employ gas-lighting, whitewashing, or do the pastors do a rewrite of the script? If they employ all these, it is their desire to control the narrative so as to be the hero or victim depending on what they set their minds to achieve. They will do anything and everything to drag you into a new reality—an alternate reality—where extremist propaganda is the only course on the menu. Their goal is to get the feeble minds. The modus operandi is always the same—manipulation.

Once they get your mind, like millions of other minds, they celebrate. Employers of gas-lighting have no interest in true information. Their whole modus operandi is repeating lies (some call it spinning) and denying reality until those whom they are targeting are convinced that the truth is a conspiracy—those spurned lies.

These spurned lies are the tools to instill fear in people so that the fearful can be controlled.
Fear as a tool is a very powerful one. With fear, you can make your enemy kiss your behind and / or toes. To say it is a remarkable logical way of thinking would be

a complete understatement. However, it is a logical way to defraud some minds.

There is a "Big Lie" in our histories. There is a "Big Lie" in our religions. Where there are no big lies, like say in statistics, then statistics is used in such a way to buttress big lies.

For this work, we will be concentrating on religions, especially those that present Heaven as a reward for good deeds on earth. The Bible was employed to justify big lies. If you can interpret the Bible correctly, you know the Bible is a book of true history.

Most people cannot interpret the Book correctly, hence the many misinterpretation and mistransliteration. Though the many misinterpretations were done through hermeneutics—the principles of bible interpretation—the Bible nevertheless was a tool for peddlers of alternative lies. The truth is still the truth even if no one believes it and a lie is still a lie even if everyone believes it.

Somewhere, in one of my books, this was written:

The Bible sounded like a tool right here. (For perspectives, I had earlier quoted Ephesians 6:5 reproduced here: **Servants, be obedient to them that are your masters according to** the flesh, with fear and trembling, in singleness of your heart, as unto Christ) *A tool for a bunch of slave masters. It sounded like a propaganda tool written by white slave masters intent on bringing some people to their knees while serving them. Only the slave masters could read and interpret the Bible for the slaves then, and they did a good job.*

One thought many people had, especially slaves—white and black slaves—was the belief they picked up from the Holy Bible . . . that there is a heaven and a hell; thus, it was really "worth the while" to fully surrender their entire life to the slave masters because the Bible so admonished. The white slaves were privileged to buy back their freedom, but the black slaves had better believe in the Bible—or be sent to an untimely hell! It was a divide-and-conquer concept unwinding.

And thus, the slaves went with the masters' call for total submission of life in slavery. Today, even after slavery, the masters still make laws that guarantee a labor supply through incarceration. They must tell you how to live . . . or else. You are not even free to make your own decisions. How can you when economic power has been taken away from you? You can't seriously rebel against the laws because some will call for you to be shot or incarcerated.

The "masters" had reasoned with the slaves using the Bible. They forced the slaves to accept that there will be some incredible rewards in heaven for those who do good works for the slave master—the rich landowner—while living here on earth. On one hand, the Bible was used to tell everyone that we were equal before God . . . while many were acquired as slaves. Oh yes, we are so equal—not on earth but in heaven. The same slaves were admonished to serve their masters on earth because their reward is in heaven.

In those times, the above big lie—deception—was deemed to be the truth. It was a lie then and it is a lie today. The lie is still a lie even if everyone believed it and practiced it. Even when those lies were laws of the time, they were still lies.

Prior and present big lies were a means to an end. The big lies are as old as the world's oldest religions. In fact, religions were manipulated by some people to invent some of the biggest lies of all times, and people fell heavily for them. The big lies—deceptions—has been a go-to modus operandi of most people seeking wealth, power, and resources for the generation of more wealth or the acquisition of more power. They strategically make up lies for profit and power.

In my book The Greatest Celestial Deception, we read and I quote:

Long ago, before we were born, greedy but powerful people had discovered that with misinformation running rampant, the truth could not be protected. Such a scenario gives cover to those seeking economic and political dominance. They have mustered the gall to dress their fearmongering, greed, deceit, and groveling under the cloak of religion. Soon, they realized that with religion, they could create a mask of lies. And they did and were very successful at it.

They never anticipated that someday, people like Robert G. Ingersoll (1833–1899) would wake up to learn about religion and conclude that "Religion can never reform mankind because religion is slavery." And even before that, another well-known, Thomas Paine (1737–1809), concluded that: ". . . I do not believe in the creed professed by the Jewish Church, by the Roman Church, by the Greek Church, by the Turkish Church, by the Protestant Church, nor by any church that I know of. My own mind is my church. Human nature is not of itself vicious."

And that is if you are assigning goodness and good deeds to and by the instructions of religions. For if you have your mind full of logic and reason, the need for religion as a guide to doing right and abstaining from bad is unnecessary. Our minds are already set to decipher good from bad. We all learn these things by the intellect.

So, sometimes, you must be diligent as well as inquisitive to bring the truth to light. People must not be allowed to change historical facts to empower their grip on social, economic, or political standing in society. Even at this hour, the spread of false information as propaganda is rampant and directly aimed at those who are most vulnerable. Fear, like love, is an emotional feeling. It is one of our animal instincts. Once you catch it, it is difficult to shed because it becomes one of your intellects. You can, however, defeat fear with the truth—the scientific facts.

The truth is available only to those who dig for it. With the truth, you then can circumvent fear. Just like Daniel J. Boorstin said: "The greatest obstacle to discovery is not ignorance—it is the illusion of knowledge." Daniel J. Boorstin went on to equivocate that: "Education is learning what you didn't even know you didn't."

And, hopefully, with courage, you can begin to question whatever you have been taught as religion and history and other related subjects. As you well know, histories, like religions, are written by the victor for the vanquished to assimilate.

Those that use fear as a weapon against you don't respect you; they despise you and expect nothing good from you. In fact, they expect the worst from you. Any attempt by you to impress them leads to an escalation of your very fears. The way it was back then and even now, the greedy and powerful learned how to use fear as a weapon. The lesson they learned and tried to implement was/is that if they are greedy and their pockets deep enough and your mind dull enough to succumb to fear, it does not matter that they are wrong. They already know that sooner or later, you would be subdued because your consciousness is already dull enough.

When you start to question what you have been made to accept as the truth, you would have abruptly discovered that those techniques back then no longer have a grip on your thought processes. The new perspective must be that if you question the "truth" enough—relearn the newly found truth enough—the greedy feeders of fear will start to lose. Their techniques to inflict fear will no longer frighten. You start to see the techniques for what they are, and their grip on you starts to loosen. The way I thought you and I must see it is: Succumbing to fear is like we are TVs and radios being muted by those that perpetrate fear.

You ultimately start to gain and they start to lose when you question the false but naïvely accepted teachings.

Ultimately, nothing limits you like your fears, and your fears shape your beliefs and behavior. Nothing controls you but your beliefs; and finally, nothing binds you and makes you who you are except your thoughts—your thoughts that are, of course, shaped—from a combination of intellects.

Since most people do not have a ladder to climb, like slaves—especially black slaves—who had no hope to climb to any height, they do not even think about climbing. Those who were entitled had hope that someday, they too could own a ladder. Today, these hopefuls are easy targets using the Big lies. You tell them to jump, they ask: How high? Today, some outlets—mostly those specializing in mass miscommunication—tells them why and how high to climb while providing them with a ladder for such a height. The height becomes hope and the big lies become the ladder with which to reach that height.

They don't care if you fatally fall off from such heights. In fact, if you fall off at such heights, you become a cost of doing business. Nothing more. Always bear that in mind before you succumb to some kind of herd mentality especially in politics and religions.

There is a wish that this work would not give you a cause for concern because if it does, you are not listening to what you are reading. If these chapters cannot convince you of the "big lies" you and I have been listening to, you are not listening to what you're reading.

Please, be reminded and be extra careful when you follow the masses because, most often, the M is silent in that word—masses. When the "M" in masses becomes silent, those are then the people you may have joined. Today, there are so many masses with the letters (m) and (e &s) missing. Do not reduce yourself to those …asses…

Chapter One   Heaven, the Perception

What is your perception of Heaven? It may not be what you had thought it was/is. This work may change your reality of what you thought Heaven is. It is likely that most readers would have their own realities about Heaven. That reality too, may likely be changed sooner than later after reading this. If you start thinking critically of Heaven; if you are shocked after reading this book, then the purpose of this work has been attained.

Most importantly, most, if not all religionists would have the same realities of Heaven. Is your reality real or is it just a mirage? Most of the questions that would be asked in this work will have answers deduced from the Holy Bible and perhaps other holy books. One question that must be answered quickly before further narrative is: Is there a Heaven?

By the Holy Bible, yes, there is a Heaven. But is the Bible's Heaven interpreted correctly? That is the real question that must be answered. When we were younger, some of us may have been brainwashed into acting as if we were put on this earth to suffer, after which, we will go to a place to receive an eternal reward of eternal enjoyment in Heaven.

Even some grown-ups, up to this day, believe strongly that there is a place of eternal enjoyment. They refer to this place as Heaven and they cite the Bible as evidence for their faith. They are working daily—doing good deeds—with faith that, one day, when they die, their reward will be that place called Heaven.

Some describe Heaven as a place where the streets are paved in gold. They opine that Heaven is so beautiful with clouds surrounding it and angels singing all day long. Heaven, they say, is a place with no pain, no sicknesses, nor death. It is a place for a never-ending angelic parties. The part where it is claimed that Heaven is surrounded by clouds might be true after all. But, what does cloud signify in that picture? This is one of the many little questions that we must take note of because it helps the readers to visualize Heaven. And visualize, you will.

There are many verses of biblical descriptions of Heaven. One very important description is that of a constant chant (watchword: constant) of holy angels that are continually proclaiming the praise line: Holy, Holy, Holy over the throne of God.

What this means is simply that God sits on His throne in Heaven where He is surrounded by magnificent angels singing His praises. Heaven, they claim, is full of the glory of God.

Using Book 1 of *A Guide to Interpreting the Bible Correctly*, can you put a finger as to the meaning of "Heaven is full of the glory of God?" Did you connect the dots and did it make any sense to you? It should make a world of sense.

And the power of God is manifest and they proclaim and praise the holy name of God without ceasing. In the preceding paragraph, please, make a note of the phrase: the glory of God. It will come up again and again, and the meaning will be made manifest.

Our planet Earth is beautiful. Look at the breathtaking views, especially from up above. You will observe how beautiful the landscape and the scenery is. There is a wow factor when you observe nature and creations. Perhaps, we assume that if Earth is this beautiful, Heaven must be spectacularly magnificent.

Heaven is perceived as a future residence for "good" souls—an eternal dwelling location—that our imagination has no ability to fathom. But, we fathom anyway. We know that Heaven is not a mythical place.

We think, and perhaps, assume that this is where the biblical God dwells. In fact, the Bible says so in many verses of the Old Testament. So, we are also told in New Testament, but we are mostly taken our evidence from the Old Testament books. According to some believers, Heaven is not a mythical place. It is the "holy" dwelling place of the Most High.

All believers say the Bible gives a delightful and beautiful descriptions of Heaven, a place where those who have received Jesus will spend eternity. They claim this because according to them, Jesus said so in John 14:2-6.
Before His death, Jesus supposedly gave His disciples a good reason why they must follow Him.

According to Jesus, He is the way, the truth, and the life, and whoever wants to live in His Father's mansions that is located in Heaven must do as He said. Perhaps, dwelling with Jesus in perpetuity is a promise and fulfilment for Christians. Below are the texts of those verses:

2 In my Father's house are many mansions: if it were not so, I would have told you. I go to prepare for you. 3 And if I go and prepare a place for you, I will come again, and receive you unto myself; that where I am, there ye may be also. 4 And whither I go ye know, and the way ye know. 5 Thomas saith unto him, Lord, we know not whither thou goest; and how can we know the way? 6 Jesus saith unto him, I am the way, the truth, and the life: no man cometh unto the Father, but by me.

At this juncture, it is recommended that you look up my book *The Greatest Celestial Deception: About the Bight Morning Star*. The book might throw some light on what or who this "Jesus" is. You may notice a big asterisk after reading *The Greatest Celestial Deception*.

If a traveler visits cities such as New York, London, Rome, Budapest, Berlin, or Ontario, he/she will see impressive-looking mansions by world's standards dotting the landscapes.

These worldly homes they will tell you, won't even come close to the perceived "mansions" Jesus have prepared for followers of Jesus, in Heaven.

Getting to Heaven, these people claim, is no picnic. You must work for it. You must follow the Ten Commandments. Apart from these commandments, you must offer your right cheek to be slapped if you were earlier smacked on the left jaw.

You are admonished to love your enemies unconditionally. You must be your brothers' keeper. You must be ready to die for this cause.

Believers in this place called Heaven, if they must get there, are encouraged to be kind and give alms to the poor. And the whopper of what must be done to get there, they preach, is to donate ten percent of their total weekly or monthly resources.

They are reminded frequently with a biblical quote of Mark 8:36.

> *For what shall it profit a man, if he shall gain the whole world, and lose his own soul?*

If you understand what a soul is, you would want to ask: how can a soul be lost when the soul does not belong to you in the first place? The soul is Consciousness. The soul is how the Intelligent Creator—Consciousness—experiences His creations through you. The soul cannot be created, destroyed or *lost*. How can God punish *Itself?* Losing one's soul is likened to punishing the all-knowing Consciousness.

The question is: is there really a Heaven? Or are the believers believing by faith? Are the preachers of the Words in the Bible correctly interpreting the "Words of God"? Is there a fog of lies in the books and is there a path out?

How do we dissolve the fog of lies if there is any? If they are making "big lies" of interpretations so as to control the narratives what could be the reason(s) for doing so? Are they doing this to control behaviors, gain power, and ultimately, the resources?

These are pertinent questions that need to be asked and answers provided. How will you react if, at the end of this book, you come to understand what Heaven really is and it isn't what you had in mind?

Hold on tight. You might be disappointed. You might feel like you've been conned. You may even feel a burden lifted off you.

Remember, realities, most often, aren't what you thought they were. This is because there is no map to reality. A religion's view of reality could be alternate reality. Or put differently, religions' reality is our ignorance because we do not understand that reality, hence we misinterpret the scriptures.

Mankind's reality is also limited.

Limited by unknown science and by what we know now. Does this reality mean that we do not know what 3+3 is? We know that 3+3 =6. We also know that reality is: up is not down. These are truths we live by. Any attempt to change these truths, therefore, is an attempt to create alternate truths. And lots of people are falling for the alternate reality as if they are on drugs that induces alternate realities.

What is your take? Think about it. The Bible has one reality. We need to understand that reality. Once you do, you begin to see how true the biblical narratives were/are.

Chapter Two
Perception of Heaven by Other Societies

Various societies/cultures do not believe in Christianity's Heaven. They believe in reincarnation. Reincarnation is a fundamental belief of most societies. What this means is that there is life after life. The Old Testament teaches that there is life after death too until Christianity rejected reincarnation for resurrection. However, that is an aside. Let's go back to Heaven.

"Heaven" is therefore either differently perceived or nonexistent. Sentient beings are believed to have the efficiency to recycle their souls forever. In fact, sentient beings can reincarnate to other planets.

It is also not a must that if you are human in this life, you must reincarnate as human. No! You can reincarnate as any life's form. Christianity's belief in a destination of either

Heaven or Hell is recent—about 2020 years ago.

An emperor thought that he had the power to make the proclamation of changing Christianity's earlier belief in reincarnation. So, he changed it. Just like other rulers and kings made changes to the original Bible. They felt like it, so, they did it—a rewrite—especially of the New Testament. Reincarnation has been acknowledged and practiced in ancient civilizations. Reincarnation is still practiced in all the continents up to this day.

Reincarnation gives the soul a chance to get it right after many tries and for as long as it takes to get it right. Christianity dictates that you have one chance to try to get it right. Your choices as a Christian, after one try, are Heaven or Hell in the afterlife. If you fail in your first life, there are no chances for redemption. You must get it right in your first experience of life on earth. You fail one time, you are doomed to Hell. That's rough and tough luck.

Societies across continents believe in veneration of ancestors (parents) who had passed. They believe that the living spring from the dead. They make elaborate yearly preparations—choosing the same times such ancestors passed on—to venerate the parents whose souls are believed to be in another dimension. Some call it: land of the dead, land of the ancestors, etc.

The reverence for the ancestors—our ancestors—is ancestor veneration. It is a recognition that the living relatives acknowledge and commemorate the roles our ancestors play in the daily lives of the living.

This practice is taken seriously in various societies for reasons we cannot fully enumerate here. We do, however, know that the elders being venerated can bless or punish those respectively that uphold societal values and those that violate societal values.

Wikipedia explained veneration of the dead thus: *The veneration of the dead, including one's ancestors, is based on love and respect for the deceased. In some cultures, it is related to beliefs that the dead have a continued existence, and may possess the ability to influence the fortune of the living. Some groups venerate their direct, familial ancestors. Certain sects and religions, in particular the Eastern Orthodox Church and Roman Catholic Church, venerate saints as intercessors with God; the latter also believes in prayer for departed souls in*

Purgatory. Other religious groups, however, consider veneration of the dead to be idolatry and a sin.

The veneration practices resonate from the understanding that the soul is Consciousness that is experiencing this universe through you. Until you meet the requirements/goals for your soul's purpose on Earth, you will continue to reincarnate to Earth. Through reincarnation, cosmic Consciousness allows all of us to see the 3D of creations.

If you want to understand the workings of reincarnation better, you may wish to read my book *Journey of The Soul*.

In some societies where there is an understanding of the Akasha, they knew all along through the Akashic Records what is and what is to be because everything is already predetermined. Therefore, whether you are bad or good is not your fault because everything you will do and say, had been predetermined.

This does not mean that one must go out of their way to do bad deeds. It does not work that way, after all, there is such a thing called karma. Or is Karma another way to describe Heaven? Heaven equation was nonexistent until recently, but alternate dimensions were existing.

In some Middle Eastern cultures, they believe in the "World to come" and accept that it is fundamental that souls recycle their existence.

In some African cultures, Asian cultures, and Mesoamerican cultures, there is an abundance of evidence in practices that echo beliefs in reincarnation.

In African Ifa/Afa divinations, a reincarnate can be exposed in minutes. The mechanisms for such divinations are still in place up until this day, to determine who has reincarnated in every new born child.

Heaven as a Tool for a Narrative: fear is a very powerful tool. A realization for a Christian that he/she may not make it to Heaven works as a powerful tool. Fear as a tool can be used to create a narrative. Fear can be a useful tool to control individuals. Religion is a tool. The fear of Hell is a frightening powerful tool.

Heaven, being the ultimate desire for every religionist become the ultimate controlling tool for the Church—the Church used to be the ultimate power base in the near ancient times. Can you imagine not being able to make Heaven?

The offensiveness of believers' past conduct—of forcing down the throats of millions of non-Catholics, and Christians who are non-Catholics, catholic beliefs—is perhaps surpassed only by the chutzpah of their current arguments for a Heaven. They know very well the impacts such a powerful tool the concepts of Heaven and Hell would be on the populace.

The fear of eternal damnation is enough to force believers to follow the teachings and interpretations offered by priests. Such interpretations/teachings can become a narrative that the particular preacher uses to force ideologies, logical or not, on the congregation.

Groups use fear for control purposes in the pursuit of power and riches. Governments worldwide use fear to intimidate. Some governments have developed "Out of this world" type of weapons with which to intimidate other governments.

From my book The Greatest Celestial Deception: About the Bright Morning Star, we read:

Perpetrators of fear, we very well know, dehumanize their victims. Sometimes perpetrators use fear in hopes of attaining a variety of set objectives.

Some can manage fear very well up to where they package and sell it. Whether you will agree you have bought into fear is debatable. In most instances, those who choose fear as a weapon are far too gone in their rabid hatred of those they despise—a group or enemy in their society.

When they come to their senses, if they ever do, they realize that they were no heroes or nationalists of their tribe or group or association. They were simply killers on the rampage to attain some greedy goals. The history of religion contains the use of force and death as punishment for nonbelievers and sinners.

By the time reason, once again, takes control of their being, the damage has already been inflicted, histories obliterated, humans savaged, and the earth we have will have been scorched beyond recognition. Most people on earth today have bought into fear, and they don't know it. It does not matter where you live; you live under some fears. Sometimes we live under the fear of our societal laws. However, the fear of our laws is not under discussion here.

If you live by religion, you have signed a mortgage— a buy into fear. Fear has been packaged and sold to you. And you bought it . . . hook, line, and sinker.

Still the same Chapter in the book we read: Perhaps the biggest fear weaponized is that of death. Heaven and hell were manufactured. Death was instituted and later osmosed into all our systems and institutions to scare the crap out of you.

The world of today, like yesterday, is/was often inhabited by fear, so much so, that national policies are dictated by fear.

Years ago, oligarchs and their enforcers were regularly and intentionally cooking up ever-malleable and watered-down truths to sow fear, not caring who or what is destroyed as they pursued those goals.

Today, lies have metamorphosed into alternative truths as if a truth of 2+2 can be something else other than 4. Ideally, truth should be an easy term to define because the truth is fact. Fact is a provable data you can rely on today or tomorrow. It stands the test of time. Up is up while down is down. Up is never down. Today, however, alternative truths have become the framework on which lies and fear are built. Today, counterfeit truths are being perpetuated by political parties and allies supported by financial benefactors, disseminated by opportunistic partisan media houses, and blessed by a faction of the clergy.

The fear of not achieving Heaven keeps almost half the world's population docile and malleable. This is a fear inflicted on you by the Church. It may be a fear instilled in you by your local pastor who encourages you to do as he/her says.

People become targets. They become controllable because now they've gotten a targeted narrative from their teachers.

So, is religion truly interpreting Heaven as a place of eternal enjoyment to entice and control its followers? If you cannot answer this question now, don't worry. Soon, you'd be able to answer it.

Is Heaven and its opposite a sort of allegories? This question is so relevant because the Bible is fond of allegorizing. The Bible also uses zoomorphism to describe things and places—be it bible characters or things.

Society as a whole is yet to understand "Game Theory." Game theory is explained as the study and understanding of mathematical models for strategic interaction among rational decision-makers.

The applications in all fields of social science, as well as in logic, systems science, and computer science helps societies and indeed mankind. Some call it the zero-sum games, in which each participant's gains or losses are exactly balanced by those of the other participants.

By this explanation, mankind is not rational enough to abide by zero-sum games. Human behavior tells us that most humans want to grab and continue to grab more power and more resources, so as to hold on to all the resources they can get for now, fearing scarcity in the future. Humans, therefore, commit all atrocities to get what they want.

Now, how many people are going to be calm enough on Earth to listen to and understand Game theory and have the patience to practice it? You think all persons will practice Game Theory? Game Theory is preaching cooperation to irrational people because human instinct is to compete. Competition brings out the best in us. It also brings the animal and the worst in human behavior. Competition can make humans murder one another to reach their goals.

Is Heaven, therefore, another word for karma? This question is suitable here because to get to "Heaven," you are admonished that there is recompense for every bad action we make against humanity. It seems that by Game Theory, it would be better for humankind to work out their differences rather than violence and other vices.

Is Heaven therefore, used as a tool to control people? Of course, yes. Whether Heaven is meant literally, as a place or a tool, will be made clear in chapters 7 & 8 where the question: Is there a Heaven—the Reality, was asked and answered.

Perhaps, "Heaven and Hell" were never meant to be thought of as literal places. Let us not be too quick to forget that the Old Testament used different sorts of allegories to describe things and places.

Heaven and Hell, therefore, could have been literarily tools to describe natural karma by allegorizing Heaven. Allegory or no allegory, Heaven is a thing, a place, but not what the Church told us it was/is.

In Chapter Four *Is there a Heaven?* Isaiah 14:12-16 was explained. Perhaps, you will glean the answer for whether Heaven and Hell are real or allegories.

Here is a question: what else in the Old Testament could you possibly think of as an allegory? If Heaven is an allegory, what about the occupants of Heaven? At the end of this book, you may very well have the answers to these questions. Hopefully!

Chapter Three
Religion as a Groupthink?

There better be a Heaven. You probably have heard people say that sentence in discussions. There is a sister to that phrase. There better be a Hell is the sister.

Most religionists are drawn to groups that believe there is a Heaven and indeed a Hell. Whether this is a Ying & Yang dualism is not ruled out at all. But then, religions cannot stand and fulfill their purposes without the dualism of good and bad, black and white, night and day, nice and evil, etc.

The core belief is that there is a life after death in Heaven where believers think they will eternally be enjoying themselves or in a Hell eternally burning up in an unquenchable fire.

Where the belief gained logicality that an immaterial soul is able to burn in a material fire is beyond this author. I will not rule out anyone somewhere chiming in to correct and complete the last sentence by saying "It is a holy fire."

The soul is an individuated consciousness. Consciousness is God—The Creator that was only mentioned in a few verses in Genesis 1. Consciousness is Awareness. Consciousness is Intelligence. Consciousness gave its Intelligence and Awareness to its creations so much so that the creations' two molecules of hydrogen "intelligently" knows how to add one molecule of oxygen and voila water is formed.

That is Consciousness' creation.

And you think that individuated consciousness can burn in such a place as a Hell? Hello! You need to start thinking differently already.

Fire is a thing, and a soul is not. Some could spin fire to be supernatural fire, but that is a spin like Heaven and Hell were products of spin and or misinterpretation. That spin was a direct concept of groupthink. Religions are like organizations and organizations do groupthink a lot.

A couple of definitions for groupthink as a thing were considered, but the Wikipedia's definition is spectacularly befitting for this work.

Wikipedia defines groupthink as: a psychological phenomenon that occurs within a group of people in which the desire for harmony or conformity in the group results in an irrational or dysfunctional decision-making outcome.

Cohesiveness, or the desire for cohesiveness, in a group may produce a tendency among its members to agree at all costs. This causes the group to minimize conflict and reach a consensus decision without critical evaluation. Janis, I. (1972).

That last sentence is very telling. Lack of critical thinking just to reach a consensus tells perhaps the best and worst thing you need to know about groupthink. There will be a few speaker(s) dishing out the commentaries/narratives while there are lots of others—perhaps in their millions—doing the listening and cowering.

Some might argue that there is no group that makes people cower in fear like religious groups. There is no group that uses fear to intimidate like religious groups, they will add. They will say that once you buy into the fear, you are doomed because you become the listener. You are not the one making some of your decisions. You've been caged in a religion groupthink.

Religion, they conclude, is simply a groupthink. But then, are we really taking into consideration the histories of various religions? Why is there so much acrimony within each group?
Perhaps, it depends on your reality. Is it really the religion that is forcing a groupthink or the people of the cloth who are interpreting the verses of the book? Think about it, if religions were creating a groupthink, how come there is a *Church and all those other churches protesting against it?*

If there was a groupthink, how come there are over 30,000 Christian denominations worldwide? Burgeoning denominations in all religions is symptomatic of disagreements—a lack of consensus.

Perhaps, there has been much critical thinking, hence there were so much rancor, disagreements, and too many sects. With all the rancor, illogical conclusions, and divisions, if somebody suggests that the cure for groupthink is religion, it will make a logical critical thinking and a good argument too.

If anything, there are more denominations and sects morphing in various locations than all the religions put together. So, though religions appear to groupthink, the religions are so far apart in ideologies, practices, beliefs, etc. than you are able to observe. The religions—all of them.

Groupthink exists in most political, economic, and social organizations. Though there is the need to reach consensus in a timely fashion, to improve co-operation, to have tasks completed timely, to improve harmony and create less conflict, it can also ruin relationships over a long period of time especially where there is strong/authoritarian leader.

Problems can be solved inefficiently because not all possibilities were considered. Innovations can be suppressed because there was a rush to reach judgment and, therefore, bad conclusion.

There must be a mechanism in place to listen to many suggestions and indeed look outside the box.

With religions, the need to look outside the box becomes even more crucial especially with all the new knowledge we have acquired in this Age of Pisces leading to the Age Aquarius.

This time (today) is radically different from the recent ancient times.

Hermeneutics—the principles of Bible interpretation—must move away from the groupthink type Bible studies and interpretations and begin to accept innovations to thoughts.

Suggestions coming from outside the box should be considered carefully. No one person or group can claim a key to the Supercomputers of this universe. The make-believe insinuations by some rogue preachers should be questioned by their congregants.

A mechanism should be put in place stipulating how the congregants should go about making suggestions that contribute to/modify the accepted practices and interpretations of that church.

They should interpret the Bible truthfully as is. Preachers must not be allowed to play "God." They should interpret correctly the authors intended meanings at all times. When people of the cloth keep making stuff up as they go, they create confusion, not clarity for the members.

Preachers should not be "thinking" for the Bible but interpret the Book correctly. If the Book is understood, they must have by now known the civilization in which the Bible's narratives took place. They must have known who or what God and His angels were/is. If the books are interpreted correctly, parishioners will need not to believe by faith only but also by proven truth.

The truth, that is the Old Testament, is history come alive.

Religious texts must be radically and truthfully interpreted as the ages' open their hidden knowledge to mankind. Misinterpretation is one reason the pages seem lost on theistic ears already dejected listening to the words coming out of the mouth of a preacher struggling to make a story line out of the texts written thousands of years ago.

While still a Christian, there are phenomena in Christian doctrines that practicing Christians are still questioning even where there is a groupthink answer. How many "religious" individuals do you know who will continually question their faith?

If they question it, it is because the foundation of their belief was laid on sands and on faith. There are Christians who question some decisions made by the Vatican, yet they remain Catholic and neither would the Church ostracize those who disagree with it.

So, the question then remains: do all religionists believe in Heaven because of groupthink? The lack of out-of-the-box thinking, the inability of followers to re-examine their presupposed beliefs with logical reasoning, and the mass monopolization of this tool of fear to manipulate people's hopes and fears make it apparently impossible for believers to believe anything else except believe that decision already reached for them through groupthink. Groupthink, therefore, becomes the basis for the foundation of their beliefs.

Chapter Four   Is There a Heaven?

If No—the Proof

Did the Bible, especially the Old Testament, ever suggest a Heaven where souls of dead people go to rest and enjoy for all eternity? It seems that there is a misinterpretation of Heaven wherever it is mentioned in the verses of the books in the Old Testament. Almost always, interpreters want to insert nonexistent things into passages.

For example, if you read Isaiah 14:12-16, how would you interpret it? This question is important because, in these five verses, the whole Bible seemed summarized. Heaven is mentioned. Hell is mentioned too.

Some people who make a living out of the study of hermeneutics might have their take which may be different from yours. However, an understanding of the principles of hermeneutics allows us to use the Bible to interpret the Bible to get at the authors' intended meanings (AIM).

Meanwhile, let us now correctly interpret those five verses by borrowing from my book *The Greatest Celestial Deception*.

Pages 85/86 had it explained. Prophet Isaiah captured the essence and thinking, of the ancients, but one needs to be able to interpret it correctly to understand that essence.

What the practices were at that time and what the writers did then was the personification of celestial bodies—the stars. The solar gods were the personification of celestial bodies as deities. Even the use of religious books of record for evidence would point to the same historical writings and depictions from ancient whispers. From the book of Isaiah 14:12–16, we read about the personification of the sun. You may wish to read the whole chapter. Let's read from the NIV:

[12] *How you have fallen from heaven, morning star, son of the dawn! You have been cast down to the earth, you who once laid low the nations!*
[13] *You said in your heart, "I will ascend to the heavens; I will raise my throne above the stars of God; I will sit enthroned on the mount of assembly, on the utmost heights of Mount Zaphon.*

¹⁴ I will ascend above the tops of the clouds; I will make myself like the Most High."
¹⁵ But you are brought down to the realm of the dead, to the depths of the pit.
¹⁶ Those who see you stare at you, they ponder your fate: "Is this the man who shook the earth and made kingdoms tremble . . ."

Here, you must have known immediately that the sun was being discussed. The movement of the sun from its celestial highest point to the lowest point was a marvel to the ancients. They were wowed! They did not understand it. So, sometimes, they worried that the sun might not appear, and when it does, it becomes such a mystery that it must be deified.

Now, I have asked some people well versed in their religious books the meaning of the above. The above verses were immediately equated with Lucifer—Satan—and the decreed punishment.

In fact, the King James Version literally translates "Morning Star" as Lucifer. Here it is:

¹² How art thou fallen from heaven, O Lucifer, son of the morning! How art thou cut down to the ground, which didst weaken the nations!
¹³ For thou hast said in thine heart, I will ascend into heaven, I will exalt my throne above the stars of God: I will sit also upon the mount of the congregation, in the sides of the north:

¹⁴ I will ascend above the heights of the clouds; I will be like the Most High.

¹⁵ Yet thou shalt be brought down to hell, to the sides of the pit.

[16] They that see thee shall narrowly look upon thee, and consider thee, saying, is this the man that made the earth to tremble . . .

What you must glean from the above are:

1. *From verse 12—"fallen from heaven" means descent of the sun.*
2. *From verse 13—"in the sides of the north"—Northern Hemisphere.*
3. *From verse 14—"Most High" literally means most high point.*
4. *From verse 15—"brought down to hell/Sheol/pit" is the lowest point that occurs on December 22nd, 23rd, and 24th.*

You may have noticed how the word heaven, heavens, and hell were used. With the interpretation provided so far, do you now understand how heaven, hell and the sun have been allegorized? Please, recognize that "heavens" equal space. Mars and the other planets are part of the heavens. If you were standing on Mars, and you look up the sky, you are looking at the heavens. Standing on Mars, our Earth becomes part of the heavens. However, "Heaven" is used in those verses for a place with a location.

The belief that Heaven is an abode for an afterlife that awaits mankind, some have described as a fairy tale designed for people afraid of death.

Some others describe Heaven as a religious invention just as they dismiss Hell as weapon created to frighten those who are inclined to do evil.

So they conclude their arguments by alluding that there will be nothing left of us, the moment our brains flickers for the last time.

Sometimes, there is this urge to remind individuals to think of the time of their conception, the time you were in the womb, and the time you were born until a few years thereafter.

Can you remember any of those times? The bottom line: there are much more we are yet to learn and comprehend. There are many realities we are yet able to fathom.

In creation, there is duality. Duality means the opposite of what is. If there is darkness, its opposite is light. Duality means hot and cold, Babyboy and Grandpa, Babyboy and baby girl, Man and Woman, light and darkness, female and male, etc.

All these dualities are creations. In every creation, there is duality. There is also the duality of birth and death. All dualities are creations. The dualities are therefore living.

Death, therefore, is alive. Death is not death. Death is living. Can science explain death? Yes, with biology. But, that is not all there is to it.

In another instance, the book of Exodus has a narrative of manna falling from Heaven. The story is accurately told of the event but interpreters are making illogical of a logical happening.

Heaven is viewed as a divine place where the LORD resides. It is a spiritual place. Manna is food made up of atoms. Atoms are material things. How can a "supposedly" immaterial Heaven suddenly show up in the horizons with material food? This is not being made up. The story is in the Bible.

Manna is food. The word manna means "what is it?" and it is a bread-like food that the Bible says fell from Heaven. It tasted like honey.

Let us lift the story from Exodus 16:1-16 and also from Psalm 78:21-30. It will be nice if the entire Chapters are read for clarity.

1 And they took their journey from Elim, and all the congregation of the children of Israel came unto the wilderness of Sin, which *is* between Elim and Sinai, on the fifteenth day of the second month after their departing out of the land of Egypt.
2 And the whole congregation of the children of Israel murmured against Moses and Aaron in the wilderness:
3 And the children of Israel said unto them, Would to God we had died by the hand of the LORD in the land of Egypt, when we sat by the flesh pots, *and* when we did eat bread to the full; for ye have brought us forth into this wilderness, to kill this whole assembly with hunger.
4 Then said the LORD unto Moses, Behold, I will rain bread from heaven for you; and the people shall go out and gather a certain rate every day, that I may prove them, whether they will walk in my law, or no.
5 And it shall come to pass, that on the sixth day they shall prepare *that* which they bring in; and it shall be twice as much as they gather daily.
6 And Moses and Aaron said unto all the children of Israel, At even, then ye shall know that the LORD hath brought you out from the land of Egypt:

7 And in the morning, then ye shall see the glory of the LORD; for that he heareth your murmurings against the LORD: and what *are* we, that ye murmur against us?
8 And Moses said, *This shall be*, when the LORD shall give you in the evening flesh to eat, and in the morning bread to the full; for that the LORD heareth your murmurings which ye murmur against him: and what *are* we? your murmurings *are* not against us, but against the LORD.
9 And Moses spake unto Aaron, Say unto all the congregation of the children of Israel, Come near before the LORD: for he hath heard your murmurings.
10 And it came to pass, as Aaron spake unto the whole congregation of the children of Israel, that they looked toward the wilderness, and, behold, the glory of the LORD appeared in the cloud.
11 And the LORD spake unto Moses, saying,
12 I have heard the murmurings of the children of Israel: speak unto them, saying, At even ye shall eat flesh, and in the morning ye shall be filled with bread; and ye shall know that I *am* the LORD your God.
13 And it came to pass, that at even the quails came up, and covered the camp: and

in the morning the dew lay round about the host.

14 And when the dew that lay was gone up, behold, upon the face of the wilderness *there lay* a small round thing, *as* small as the hoar frost on the ground.

15 And when the children of Israel saw *it*, they said one to another, It *is* manna: for they wist not what it *was*. And Moses said unto them, This *is* the bread which the LORD hath given you to eat.

16 This *is* the thing which the LORD hath commanded, Gather of it every man according to his eating, an omer for every man, *according to* the number of your persons; take ye every man for *them* which *are* in his tents.

You may wish to read the rest of the chapter for the whole story and for context.

Meanwhile, the book of Psalms confirms the story too. Psalm 78:21-30 is quoted below. Please compare and contrast as both stories are supposedly written at different times yet are similar.

21 Therefore the LORD heard *this*, and was wroth: so a fire was kindled against Jacob, and anger also came up against Israel;
22 Because they believed not in God, and trusted not in his salvation:
23 Though he had commanded the clouds from above, and opened the doors of heaven,
24 And had rained down manna upon them to eat, and had given them of the corn of heaven.
25 Man did eat angels' food: he sent them meat to the full.
26 He caused an east wind to blow in the heaven: and by his power he brought in the south wind.
27 He rained flesh also upon them as dust, and feathered fowls like as the sand of the sea:
28 And he let *it* fall in the midst of their camp, round about their habitations.
29 So they did eat, and were well filled: for he gave them their own desire;
30 They were not estranged from their lust. But while their meat *was* yet in their mouths,

People who may have read the book *A Guide to Interpreting the Bible Correctly* might have understood, seen through their mind's eye, and translated the event that was taking place.

The Bible (Old Testament) tells its stories in straight forward manner. There is, however, the need to understand the allegories, zoomorphism, etc.

Allegories are almost always symptomatic of the problems that would arise in a transliteration of the Bible. Whether this was a means for misrepresentation or misinformation/disinformation by those doing the interpreting is open for debate. This is because if one understands the authors' intended meaning (AIM), the Bible comes "alive" when reading its stories.

In all the verses above, one can pick out a few code words from a few of the verses. When the dots are connected and the knots tied, the clear picture of the story emerges.

From Ex. 16:4; 16:7; & 16:10
Verse 4 have the words "*rain bread* from *heaven.*"
Verse 7: There was *the glory of the LORD appeared in the cloud.*
Verse 10: The glory of the LORD

From Psalm 78:13; 78:24; & 78:25. You are encouraged to read the entire Psalm 78 to get a clearer picture.

From verse 13, there are the words *clouds,* and *doors of heaven.* The two words literally mean exactly what they mean today. There were no other meanings assigned other than what they stand for. It is the doors to a UFO—unknown flying object—in the clouds.
Verse 24: Has the texts *"rained down Manna."* To make this come alive, if you picture in your mind's eye, a cargo plane dropping its cargo from the clouds of Manna/food.
Verse 25: Comes with "Angel's food." Literally means the angels prepped and rained the area where the congregants occupied with food which the extraterrestrials themselves ate.

The *glory of the LORD* is an aircraft just like *heaven*. The difference is in size. Take cognizance that this heaven has doors. Picture an army dropping cargo or food from a jumbo cargo aircraft to people on the ground from the cloud. That was all there was to it. This was a depiction of an event where "God" and His angels—extraterrestrials—devised a way to feed a hungry people. And they repeated this for six days in a week.

Chapter Five   Heaven as another Dimension?

If by Heaven, it means another dimension, perhaps, that makes it reasonable even if the believer is believing by faith. Not even Solomon the Wise was very confident if there was another dimension. The Bible in the book of Ecclesiastes talks about death. Several verses in the book of Ecclesiastes seem to suggest that even King Solomon seemed not to understand *afterlife.* In fact, there are some believers who quote the book of Ecclesiastes to suggest that the soul dies like the body. And that God will recreate the person later on the day of resurrection.

Well, believers are entitled to their beliefs. But an understanding of the soul as an energy, that can neither be created nor destroyed, creates a logical pathway to reincarnation.

The soul is Consciousness experiencing the material world through living and even inanimate things. Stones as inanimate things, have energy too. Therefore, a soul is never recreated.

Does Ecclesiastes actually suggest no afterlife? Chapter 3:17-22 says

17 I said in mine heart, God shall judge the righteous and the wicked: for *there is* a time there for every purpose and for every work.
18 I said in mine heart concerning the estate of the sons of men, that God might manifest them, and that they might see that they themselves are beasts.
19 For that which befalleth the sons of men befalleth beasts; even one thing befalleth them: as the one dieth, so dieth the other; yea, they have all one breath; so that a man hath no preeminence above a beast: for all *is* vanity.
20 All go unto one place; all are of the dust, and all turn to dust again.
21 Who knoweth the spirit of man that goeth upward, and the spirit of the beast that goeth downward to the earth?
22 Wherefore I perceive that *there is* nothing better, than that a man should rejoice in his own works; for that *is* his portion: for who shall bring him to see what shall be after him?

If you read the first few verses, it was clear that King Solomon is talking about what befalls our bodies when we die. The physical body he opined will die and decompose like animal body. It looks like the King is at a loss as to why humans were not above animals.

The final verse does not explicitly suggest that our soul (including animal soul and indeed all souls) also dies. The King was indeed seeking answers to where the soul resides after our bodies were incapacitated.

The King was, in effect, saying that we do not know what happens after we die. He, therefore, advices mankind to: live your life to the fullest while you can because, according to him, death is the end-all-to human and animal bodies.

If you think about it, this is King Solomon who was known for his legendary wisdom, yet, he knew not about afterlife. Some use this lack of knowledge about afterlife for why the New Testament came to be—a clarification of the Old Testament. That will be a topic for discussion but at another time.

The book of Ecclesiastes has a verse in the beginning of the book that goes like this: *Vanity of vanities, saith the Preacher, vanity of vanities; all is vanity.*

What do you think King Solomon meant? That all is vanity? That this life now is it? That there is no afterlife? This seems to be the theme of the book of Ecclesiastes.

King Solomon, like everybody else, is pondering the afterlife. With all the powers and wisdom the angels bestowed on King Solomon, he was lacking the understanding of other dimensions. King Solomon, perhaps, wasn't just the only one thinking about this fact of life.

Live not as though there were a thousand years ahead of you. Fate is at your elbow; make yourself good while life and power are still yours. ~ Marcus Aurelius

Perhaps, King Solomon was thinking along those lines before even Marcus Aurelius, but hey, life is fleeting.

Make of it what you can because it will end soon, even before a blink of an eye. Why even worry? Death is not the end of life in whatever way you look or understand it.

In my book *Immaterial Existence* parts of Chapter 3 titled Life & Reincarnation, discussed afterlife. Below are parts of that discussion with little or no modifications for clarity.

Life is a software that requires a hardware to function. Life requires a body to manifest. In other words, the program (life) cannot manifest without a body (hardware). Every manifested life has a body. The body could be human, a dog, monkey, grasshopper, ant, termite, fish, earthworm, plant, etc.

All the above mentioned bodies, or hardware, have their DNA with minuscule differences. They are the hardware life uses. When the hardware becomes corrupted and of no use any longer, then life leaves that hardware and seeks new hardware. This process of manifesting in a new body is what some cultures refer to as reincarnation. What or who is it exactly that becomes reincarnated?

The theosophical point of view holds that spiritual evolution extends through reimbodiments, or reincarnations. This can be repeatedly done for humans and all living things, including animals and plants. Indeed, it can be done for all things from a subatomic level to the realm of the galaxies.

From the Akashic Records, we know that there is a finite number of human souls. Few of these are incarnate at any given time. The Akashic Records contain all that will happen or not happen for all reincarnates.

We also read extensively the workings of reincarnation.

Reincarnation has as its core ideology in the recycling of the spirits. Some religions like Hinduism have added the element of Karma to it as well to further build on the belief of reincarnation. It is a core part of many religions, including most of the African traditional religions.

The concept of conservation of energy states that energy can be neither created nor be destroyed, but can be transformed from one form to another. For instance, chemical energy can be converted to kinetic energy in the explosion of a stick of dynamite. A consequence of the law of conservation of energy is that a perpetual motion machine of the first kind cannot exist. This applies to its spiritual parallel. Life is nothing, yet life is everything. Life is everlasting because spiritual energy is the soul. Life cannot be destroyed, but if the hardware is destroyed, life is forever looking for another piece of hardware (body).

Christianity alludes to an everlasting life whether in heaven or in hell, but that is another way of alluding to life in another dimension.

Some people would want you to believe that the whole thrust of the Bible opposes reincarnation. They argue that the Bible talks resurrection—not reincarnation. They want to convince you that man is the special creation of God—in God's own image with both a material body and an immaterial soul.

Life needs a body to manifest. Per this argument, man is presented as distinct and unique from all other creatures—angels and the animal kingdom alike.

The Bible teaches that at death, man's body which is mortal, decays and returns to dust. His soul/spirit continues either in a place of torment for those who are "sinners" or in a "paradise" with God. Again, whether heaven or hell or a world-to-come, it is an affirmation of a belief in other dimensions. However, a major distinction is that in Christianity, they propose two types of death: the death of the body and the death of the soul.

Christianity, in effect, peddles the teaching that a living body might have a dead soul. In other words, when the living body dies, so does the soul. Therefore, the soul can only have an afterlife after the resurrection that only can be achieved through belief in Jesus Christ. That logic is perpetuated in the rapture theology of the so-called born-again Christians.

Indeed, many world religions portray that although a body is alive, the soul within that body may be dead and remains dead. The Bible, and, indeed, the Koran, teaches, or implies, that although people seem to be alive, their souls may be dead.

Other religions have taken it a notch higher by implying that only dead people's souls reincarnate. What this means is that as far as there is reincarnation, it only signifies that the reincarnating soul was/is dead, for if it was not dead, it will be resurrected. Thus, reincarnation will continue until resurrection occurs, thereby breaking the wheel of Samsara. Samsara (Sanskrit) is the repeating cycle of birth, life, and death—reincarnation—as well as a person's actions and its consequences in the past, present, and future. This belief is found within Hinduism, Buddhism, Bon, Jainism, Taoism, and Sikhism.

Christianity, however, promises a presence in heaven for those who have trusted in the Savior. They will be resurrected to eternal life with a glorified body (John 5:25–29).

The emphatic teaching of Heb. 9:27 in the New Testament is that "It is appointed unto men once to die and after that the judgment." The word to watch here is "once," meaning that you live once and die once. It leaves no room for reincarnation. Thus, the concept that mankind's creation in God's image is unique from the animals, and even angels stand totally opposed to the idea of reincarnation—dying and coming back as another living thing.

For most people, life is described as: the condition that distinguishes animals and plants from inorganic matter, including the capacity for growth, reproduction, functional activity, and continual change preceding death.

Or: the existence of an individual human being or animal.

Or: the period between the birth and death of a living thing.

Does that describe life for you as an individual?

Someone told me that life is nothing. She went ahead to explain that when you were born, you knew nothing, and when you died, you never knew you died. What caught my fancy and why I mentioned that someone, is that she mentioned the word "nothing."

"Nothing" is the greatest word. If you knew what "nothing" is, you will never ever tell anyone that they are nothing. For though nothing is nothing, yet nothing is everything.

Humans are not life, nor are animals and trees. Life existed before humans, animals, and plants. Life will continue to exist if there are no humans, animals, and plants. Humans, animals, and plants are just the avenues for life to manifest.

The Gods told us the truth. The problem is that some people have turned that truth into a divine lie to make man docile and malleable, perhaps to instill the fear of the authorities. Where possible, the lies were turned into a moneymaking scheme.

In the Old Testament, the Gods, through their actions—the big flood—wiped mankind out of the land. So, you think that those who were killed then, if they were to meet the Gods in heaven, would they not ask why they killed them all? The point being that the Gods knew then that there was no heaven or hell. They too were susceptible to nature's wrath.

They had bodies like us, and they told us so.

If you have a knowledge for the creation of man, you will marvel at the deception the fabrication of a heaven has caused for mankind. The Gods needed man, so man was created/re-engineered. Man did not need the Gods. Man was still evolving.

Supreme Intelligence has designed and timed man and put mankind on a course to evolve to a higher echelon on earth. You may wish to read my book Why Was Man Created? When you do, you would not fall to that same deception applied for the introduction and belief in hell or heaven.

Hell was/is simply made up. Hell, or heaven, is a concocted misnomer. The biblical Gods could not have been advocating a location of somewhere called heaven. We know this because we know the purpose of man was to serve under them. How could they have created heaven where man would enjoy eternal days after earth's sojourn when the Gods themselves have a destiny with death too?

Perhaps, we as humans, are the ones making Gods up because we understand far less during the times of those "Gods." They were not Gods. And you better believe it because they were extraterrestrials, after all, with bodies like ours. They did not deceive us because they told us in simple terms: Let Us make man in our image and likeness.

They lived for thousands of years as recorded in some archaeological finds. Like Enoch, they lived long years. Like Adam, they lived thousands of years.

Like Eve, most of their siblings lived thousands of years.

Archaeological findings are also bearing testimony to these facts. If you understand the characteristics of the Gods, you will quickly see why they never, in any fashion whatsoever, advocated or gave the impression that there is a place known as heaven. Like hell, heaven was not mentioned as part of creation. Heavens must not be confused for heavens in the narratives of creation in Gen. 1:1.

The Old Testament promised no such place as heaven. In fact, the Gods specified where man shall return after death. In Genesis 3:19, we read:

In the sweat of thy face shalt thou eat bread, till thou return unto the ground; for out of it was thou taken: for dust thou art, and unto dust shalt thou return.

There was no promise of heaven in the quote above. It is self-explanatory. Perhaps, they saw such proclamation as a punishment. If you also know who these Gods were, you would not even give them the adulation that our forefathers gave them because they had all the qualities of man—good and bad—or worse. They too believe in a higher being—the Universal Creator. The One referred to here also as Consciousness, Supreme Creator, Supreme Intelligence, etc.

In the very first words of the Bible, the biblical lords—no matter the names they chose to be recognized by—acknowledged the Universal Creator and narrated His first creation, which are the heavens and the earth. The heaven(s) is nothing but space and all things that would emanate from space. From Genesis 1:1, we read:

In the beginning, God created the heavens and the earth.

Bear in mind that the writers of Genesis wrote Genesis based on their understanding of yet another narrative. Somebody borrowed heavily from the Sumerian clay tablets. The writer(s) did not have the luxury of the sciences like we have today. We now know that the heavens and Earth were not created at the same time or simultaneously. We know through science that the heavens (space) came into existence many, many billions of years before Earth formed.

If heaven was created at the time Earth was created, how come there is limited or no mention of it in the Old Testament? Don't even pay any mind to those who would regurgitate Gen. 1:1 as evidence of heaven's mention. That heaven or heavens, depending on the Bible version you are using, simply means the sky and/or space but not a particularly designated place of enjoyment where a "God" is sitting on a throne waiting to be venerated all day and all night.

There is not a lot in the Old Testament about heaven except to say that it is the abode of the God(s). To say it is the abode of the Gods is a factual statement because the extraterrestrials arrived from and departed to space. So, if our forefathers described space as the Gods' abode, they were not hallucinating. They are factually correct.

In most, if not all of the instances, those who are said to have had visions of heaven seem to not have the appropriate words to describe it. Let us note some of the foundational truths about heaven as was revealed in scripture. It is the accepted teaching that heaven is the spiritual realm in which the glory of God's presence is revealed, and in which dwell the angels of God, and all believers who have departed this world (Heb. 12:22–24).

22 But ye are come unto mount Sion, and unto the city of the living God, the heavenly Jerusalem, and to an innumerable company of angels,
23 To the general assembly and church of the firstborn, which are written in heaven, and to God the Judge of all, and to the spirits of just men made perfect,
24 And to Jesus the mediator of the new covenant, and to the blood of sprinkling, that speaketh better things than that of Abel.

The Gods employed covenants as the coercive force to achieve their aims. They never employed deception, deception as in the use of a place called heaven. What are covenants, and why did the Gods use them to instill fear in humans? If you have read the book Why Was Man Created?—one of my books—you would have immediately known that the Gods do not want your worship. If no worship, therefore, no heaven. After all, were we not indoctrinated in a belief that we were created to worship and praise God so that when we die, we resurrect and live in heaven thereafter?

Heaven is made out to look like a very short skirt worn by hookers to attract their victims. Once the fuse of the heaven canister was lit, it has been on fire ever since. The lure of heaven was also employed in our not-so-distant past for propaganda in conquest of continents. The promise of heaven and hell through religious teachings was heavily employed to subdue slaves.

The advocators of heaven fully understood the importance of indoctrination. The gullible are fascinated with the heaven-and-hell dichotomy, while hoping for a return on investment that is an eternal enjoyment in heaven and avoidance of damnation in hell.

Some have fathomed that the idea of heaven is the most forceful weapon against traditional indigenous religions in continents they wish to conquer. Even as they propagate heaven, they know and regard Christianity as one of the most fatal and seductive lies that has ever existed. Sometimes, you wonder why Christians believe much more so in the doctrine of heaven and hell. So much so than the believers who use the book, Torah.

I have always thought that the Jews do not believe in the concept of hell. A further investigation revealed that there is not a definitive understanding of life after death—not even is it definitive as in heaven or hell. There has never been one definitive understanding of life after death because, understandably, there is a difference between what "Jews" believe versus what "Judaism" says. I have personally heard a Jew say that there is no God. I was shocked, even though at that time I was one being goaded as a Christian.

Jews may or may not believe in the afterlife—no heaven, no hell, no anything—Judaism, however, unequivocally does. While reading some literature, I came to an understanding that Jews don't believe in life after death. No hell. No nothing. No heaven.

However, when you widen your horizon and do some research, as you would on everything else, you will quickly learn to separate what Jews believe and what Judaism teaches. Although there are specks in modern Judaism that teach no afterlife, Judaism, in most instances, including Jewish theology, Jewish history, unequivocally believes in Olam Habah—the world-to-come.

So, you might want to ask: where, then, is this world-to-come? Is that the heaven?

Yes, there is heaven in Judaism. Although the Hebrew Bible devoted little to no time in speculating about heaven or hell, there are many instances where you can read of other dimensions in the Hebrew and Christian Bibles.

Let us look at one of those instances in the book of 1 Sam. 28:1–25. The lesson to draw here is that Samuel the prophet was already dead and buried.

King Saul heard the prophet as he delivered the painful and sorrowful message from the other dimension. What you should take out from this encounter is to ask yourself: what dimension was Prophet Samuel speaking from? There was another dimension, and Prophet Samuel was in it.

Let's read a few verses from that chapter. You may wish to read the whole chapter (from the NRSVCE).

[11] Then the woman said, "Whom shall I bring up for you?" He answered, "Bring up Samuel for me." [12] When the woman saw Samuel, she cried out with a loud voice; and the woman said to Saul, "Why have you deceived me? You are Saul!" [13] The king said to her, "Have no fear; what do you see?" The woman said to Saul, "I see a divine being coming up out of the ground." [14] He said to her, "What is his appearance?" She said, "An old man is coming up; he is wrapped in a robe." So, Saul knew that it was Samuel, and he bowed with his face to the ground, and did obeisance.

[15] Then Samuel said to Saul, "Why have you disturbed me by bringing me up?" Saul answered, "I am in great distress, for the Philistines are warring against me, and God has turned away from me and answers me no more, either by prophets or by dreams; so, I have summoned you to tell me what I should do." [16] Samuel said, "Why then do you ask me, since the LORD has turned from you and become your enemy?"

Though the Hebrew Torah devotes little or no time to address heaven, hell, and life after death, the Jewish tradition is full of varying depictions of what the world-to-come might mean, just like the example we previously mentioned. Some notions imagine God as Avenu Malkenu—the Father and King—sitting in judgment and delivering reward or punishment within the heavenly circle where he sits in the middle of that circle. There are other notions, one of which imagines a supernal Beit Midrash—House of Study— where the Tzaddikim—the Righteous—study the Torah all day long. There are more mystical beliefs. There are the ones where Jewish traditions envision a ladder of consciousness. At the top of the ladder resides the ineffable—God beyond description. As one descends the ladder, there is a distinction that sets in with archangels, angels, spirits, and other divine beings all the way down this planet Earth where souls are coming and going. And then, there is the Jewish notion of reincarnation—returning to this world once again. In summary, there are three types of world-to-come.

    a. Garden of Eden (spiritual place)
    b. The world of souls
    c. Resurrection of the dead/reincarnation

Jewish tradition has notions on hell, too. There is, however, no one depiction of the world on high or below. It is for the purposes of reincarnation and other dimensions that the Jewish notions of hell or heaven were examined.

In African traditional religion, there are

b. The land of the spirits otherwise called the world of souls and

c. The reincarnation

a. The Garden of Eden is missing. The closest to a Garden of Eden is the land of the spirits.

Simply put, African traditional religion explains that there are dimensions in the afterlife. When certain requirements are met, souls can then reincarnate to bodies of newborn babies, mostly of extended families. After death, burial ceremonies include preparation rites before burial so that the soul would reincarnate quickly with his/her people.

Chapter Six   Gathered With His Fathers

This expression is widely used in the Old Testament when elders die. They are said to have joined their ancestors in the land of the dead.
The phrase "Gathered with his fathers" is, therefore, used to describe where the dead go to for eternal rest. This phrase has been explained in the book *Immaterial Existence* on Chapter 3:

The phrase seems to confirm the Jewish, and, in fact, some African, beliefs. The phrase was used to describe what occurs after death. The phrase, "gathered to his people," is found recorded at the death of many Old Testament notables, such as:

- Abraham (Gen. 25:7)

- Ishmael (Gen. 25:17)
- Isaac (Gen. 35:29)
- Jacob (Gen. 49:33)
- Aaron (Num. 20:24)
- Moses (Deut. 32:50)
- Josiah (2 Kgs. 22:50)

Also, the destiny of Moses was described in Deuteronomy 31:16 when the LORD said to Moses, "Soon you will lie down with your ancestors." This means Moses will rest with his fathers. This could not possibly refer to his physical body, for it was buried in a valley in the land of Moab, opposite Beth Peor (Deut. 34:6).

*It was not resting in Mamre where Abraham and Sarah (his foreparents) were buried.
After the death of Joshua, we find that an entire "generation had been gathered to their fathers" (Judg. 2:10).*

It is notable and significant to ask if the phrase was used after the death of Adam. It was not used. Can you understand why? But what exactly does it mean to be gathered to our people? "Gathered" is defined as "to be collected, gathered together," a reference used to describe the entering into Hades.

The New Testament use of Hades builds on its Hebrew parallel, Sheol, which was the preferred translation in the Septuagint. In the Old Testament, Sheol refers primarily to death and the abode of the dead. Hades, whatever dimension that is, is where the Hebrews regarded as the gathering abode of their ancestors.

This gathering to one's fathers, or one's people, is distinguished both from death and burial.

This expression implies an equal status of all those who have died—regardless of religion. Some have advanced this expression as one more piece of evidence in favor of "soul sleep." Some have argued that this expression is inconsistent with the notion of an unconscious or conscious intermediate state.

With the expression—gathered to your fathers— different people have used it to argue their positions on beliefs in opposite directions and mostly to support that position they deem fit.

Though Ancient Near Eastern traditions and African traditions do contain a great deal of talk on life after death, there is not sufficient evidence to conclude that these expressions about being gathered to one's fathers are affirming that tradition or whether the expression is affirmation of a dimension—heaven, hell, or anything.

After one understands thoroughly who the Gods are, it is very difficult to affirm with any degree of certainty that those who take these expressions as providing certainty of life after death appear to be reading that idea into these texts. Some opponents of unconscious or conscious intermediate state would approach these expressions more exegetically, and rightly so.

It will be helpful, at this juncture, to delve into who the Gods are. How much do you understand about the Gods, or are you one of those that simply believed the God you were told was a "God of war" or the

"God visiting the inequities on nine generations for the sins of their fathers"?

When you hear the word "God," what immediately comes to your mind? And when you hear the word "consciousness," what strikes you? By now, you must have understood the use of consciousness and what or who it is in this book, thus far.

The fact of the matter is that the truth was lost in translation and transliteration of the Enumah Elish and Bible texts. For example, in Exodus 20:3, it was said that:

You shall have no other gods before Me.

Some failed to understand that: as "there are other Gods besides Yahweh," and when in Exodus 20:5,

You shall not worship them or serve them; for I, the LORD your God, am a jealous God, visiting the iniquity of the fathers on the children, on the third and the fourth generations of those who hate Me . . .

In that verse, there was a corrective word to worship and it is "serve." There has been much argument in translation of the word "worship." The argument has been whether that word meant work ship and/or worship. You will not begin to understand it if you do not know why and how humans were created in the first place.

The point that you must get from this is simply that the Gods did not create you—to glorify and worship them. That is so far removed from their intentions for humans. If worshipping and glorifying them was their intent, why did they wipe mankind off the face of the earth in the great deluge then?

Now, this may bring you to asking: What are we? What is our purpose here? Or are we something else? The answers to these questions are multidimensional, and we will be discussing dimensions in the next chapter.

Chapter Seven Other Dimensions?

Humans cannot see beyond this dimension. Even in this dimension, our ability to see is limited. Our ability to see other spectrums is limited even with the help of material instruments like microscopes and telescopes.

Dimensions, as a topic, was discussed in my book *Immaterial Existence: No map to Reality*. Let us read parts of Chapter 4 which are quoted below with little or no modifications for clarity purposes.

Dreams are the gateway to other dimensions. Many people have offered explanations for dreams. Science has also offered some explanations. How science came to its conclusions is debatable, but we shall come back to that later if there is available space. It is, however, not my intention to explain the intricacies of dreams through psychology. It is my intention to look at dreams through spirituality.

Dream is the superhighway to another realm—a dimension science cannot explain yet. Any explanation thus far from the sciences is speculative. Some people dream every week. Some dream many times a week. And when you slip into dreams, you do it while asleep. Your physical body lies resting as you find a replica of yourself doing all those things you can do while not sleeping, and much more. The ability to have an out-of-body experience (dreaming) can be repetitive. When it is repetitive, your conscious and/or your unconscious is trying to pass on a message.

Whether you understand the message is another thing to worry about. Sometimes, the experiences experienced in that realm affect the physical body. For example, if one is running or engaged in a tedious fight in the spiritual realm, it is not uncommon for the physical body to start to sweat. Emotions expressed in the spiritual realm like weeping or laughing can be experienced in our dimension—this world—to the extent you notice a sleeping person crying or laughing in their sleep.

Sometimes, you are in flight—something your physical being cannot do. You can do many things your physical body cannot do in this new realm. When you enter dreamland, an insane, unstructured realm where there are no rules and no constraints—where everything is possible and where the limits of your imagination are pushed beyond infinity—is possible.

Sometimes, in dreams, you have total power, and sometimes, no power at all. You can fly, walk through walls, you can walk on water, and you can understand and infer a thousand tongues and inferences.

By far, one the best experiences in your dreams is the ability to communicate with people who are long gone. Many dreamers see and communicate with their bygone relatives. Messages received in dreams, if well interpreted and understood, have come to pass in the physical world.

The real question about dreams is: Which of you is dreaming? The body here on earth, or the one in the realm? You do not need anyone to explain to you that you already exist in another realm. You see yourself in that dimension almost always. You hear yourself talk, you see yourself even do things you cannot do on earth, and in that other dimension, your ability to see multidimension is total. That is why you see people that have passed from this earthly dimension in the multidimension.

We are living in two worlds, and the two worlds are real when you are in any of them. The experience of dreaming helps you see that we are more than our physical body, and that we are living in two worlds—the physical and the dream dimensions.

When we are in any one of these dimensions, we generally disregard the other. Just as a reminder, you will notice that certain functions of your system work automatically on their own. Your brain did not leave the function of breathing to you. If that was the case, you will stop breathing while you are asleep. There are lots of other functions the Supreme Intelligence took away from you, and such functions include that of the reflex. When we wake up in the morning and as soon as we open our eyes, we begin to engage in our physical world. The dream dimension is only a distraction in the physical world.

Or can we also say that the physical world is only a distraction in the dream world? To answer that question is difficult, because if you consider the question: which of you is dreaming? Is it the you in the physical world or the you in the dream dimension? Remember that whenever you are in one dimension, it becomes your reality.

In other words, our dream dimension may no longer be real, but only seconds ago, it was our reality, being, and existence.

The heavens—space—is the biblical name for the spiritual world that exists in parallel to the physical world. Whereas there is a multidimensional universe, we can only see the three dimensions of physical space, plus time. Some of us do assume that that is all that exists. The spiritual dimensions consist of many more dimensions of reality beyond what we can see as humans.

While alive here on earth, your superhighway to a multidimensional universe is through dreams. Have you noticed that you do not have control over how your dreams end? Why not? The idea of explaining the concept of dreams here is to expand on the reality of realms. It is not to be misunderstood for heaven or hell dimensions but to cement unto your mind the idea of dimensions. Whatever you choose to call them—hell, purgatory, afterlife, or heaven is your choice.

You may have an understanding and know the importance of different dimensions, but one place that discussed dimensions, especially the dream superhighway, is the Bible. Let us look at a few snippets from the Bible. (All verses are from NRSVCE.)

Daniel 2:1 In the second year of Nebuchadnezzar's reign, Nebuchadnezzar dreamed such dreams that his spirit was troubled and his sleep left him.

Daniel 2:28 but there is a God in heaven who reveals mysteries, and he has disclosed to King Nebuchadnezzar what will happen at the end of days. Your dream and the visions of your head as you lay in bed were these:

Daniel 2:19 Then the mystery was revealed to Daniel in a vision of the night, and Daniel blessed the God of heaven.

Here, the king and Daniel had to go to the realm through dreams to hear from a God who too was in that realm. In fact, Daniel could not have had the meaning to the dream if he did not have dreams where he received the meaning in that realm where the king received the warnings.

Yet, in another instance, the three wise men were also warned in a dream about the intentions of Herod regarding the birth of Jesus.

Some scientists often describe dreams as the attempt by the brain to recalibrate. They say that dreaming is strictly random brain impulses where our brains are working through issues from our daily life while we sleep as a sort of coping mechanism. You can make your own judgment based on the above examples of dreams in the Bible. There are more examples.

Matthew 2:12–13 And having been warned in a dream not to return to Herod, they left for their own country by another road.

[13] Now after they had left, an angel of the Lord appeared to Joseph in a dream and said, "Get up, take the child and his mother, and flee to Egypt, and remain there until I tell you; for Herod is about to search for the child, to destroy him.

One of the Bible's famous dreams we like to quote was that of a pharaoh in Egypt, Gen. 41:1–7 and Gen. 41:25:

After two whole years, Pharaoh dreamed that he was standing by the Nile, [2]and there came up out of the Nile seven sleek and fat cows, and they grazed in the reed grass. [3]Then seven other cows, ugly and thin, came up out of the Nile after them, and stood by the other cows on the bank of the Nile. [4]The ugly and thin cows ate up the seven sleek and fat cows. And Pharaoh awoke. [5]Then he fell asleep and dreamed a second time; seven ears of grain, plump and good, were growing on one stalk. [6]Then seven ears, thin and blighted by the east wind, sprouted after them. [7]The thin ears swallowed up the seven plump and full ears. Pharaoh awoke, and it was a dream.

[25]Then Joseph said to Pharaoh, "Pharaoh's dreams are one and the same; God has revealed to Pharaoh what he is about to do."

Do those dreams seem like random brain impulses, where our brains are working through our daily issues and/or trying to recalibrate itself? These are clear examples of people being able to attain various dimensions even while sleeping and alive.

You see, the subconscious mind is a very powerful thing. When the conscious mind is provided with plenty of data while awake, it absorbs it.

Then, the subconscious mind would process and make sense of that data while you are asleep. Some of the greatest scientific discoveries that make living comfortable today were made in dreams. These discoveries are a testament to the importance of the ability to tap into the dream dimension. In that dimension, we can communicate with others. Those "others" (whatever you want to call them) have learned to teach us stuff from that dimension. Let us just consider two examples of dreamers learning from that other dimension.

One was of the man, Srinivasa Ramanujan. Srinivasa is credited with thousands of new mathematical ideas; yet, he had negligible formal training in mathematics. He had over 4,000 proofs, identities, conjectures, and equations in pure mathematics. Srinivasa described the experiences as:

"While asleep, I had an unusual experience. There was a red screen formed by flowing blood, as it were. I was observing it. Suddenly, a hand began to write on the screen. I became all attention. That hand wrote several elliptic integrals. They stuck to my mind. As soon as I woke up, I committed them to writing."

Another is that of the man credited with the discovery of the periodic table. Dmitri Mendeleev was obsessed with finding a logical way to organize the chemical elements. This consumed him for months. Finally, he found himself in another dimension while asleep. When he awoke, he had the solution given to him in his dream. This was what he had to say:

"In a dream, I saw a table where all the elements fell into place as required. Awakening, I immediately wrote it down on a piece of paper."—Dmitri Mendeleev, 1834–1907

The Chapter then points to and explained the kinds of professionals who today still have access to different dimensions. Perhaps, this might seem illogical and magical, but this is so because our sciences simply cannot explain immaterial existences.

As you can see from the two examples above, all kinds of people have access to these other dimensions. Whether they choose to call these dimensions by such names as "heaven," "hell," "purgatory," or "world-to-come" is not anyone's prerogative. But there is a certainty that other dimensions exist. Many educated people, talented persons, imams, pastors, Ifá priests, shamans, medicine men, etc., talk about these dimensions, sometimes, secretly for fear of ridicule.

However, there are sets of persons who can communicate with the other dimensions when the conditions are conducive, even while not asleep. Let us look at a few.

Shamanism: *A shaman is an individual having access to, and influence in, other world dimensions. Such individuals are capable of communication with benevolent and malevolent spirits. A shaman typically enters a trance state during a ritual where he/she practices divination and healing. Shamanism, therefore, is a practice that involves a practitioner reaching altered states of consciousness to perceive and interact with another world dimension. Information and transcendental energies gained during such interaction are then channeled into helping people on this planet. Like a pastor, an Ifá priest, or a medicine man, a shaman is a person who acts as an intermediary between the natural and supernatural worlds (the different world dimensions), using information gathered from the supernatural world to cure illnesses. They can also foretell the future and control spiritual forces. Shamans can engage in discussions with the other dimension.*

Ifá priests/priestesses: *Ifá is a practice and system of divination. Ifá/Afá is mainly an African practice but has been exported through slaves to the Americas. Today, Ifá practices play a critical role in the traditional indigenous religions and the many variations of Santeria traditions of the Americas. Some overzealous persons who hardly understand the practice are quick to refer to it as voodoo. However, the Ifá divination system was added in 2005 by UNESCO to its list of the Masterpieces of the Oral* *and Intangible Heritage of Humanity. This does not mean that Ifá/Afá practices waited for some recently born organization to give it credence. Ifá practice was credible before the sciences came into existence. If anything, the Ifá practice was the channel of scientific inventions.*

The Ifá/Afá priests or priestesses act as an intermediary between the natural and supernatural worlds. Like their shaman counterparts, they use information gathered from the supernatural dimension for the betterment of mankind. What has been established here by the priests is that there are other dimensions. They tap into these other dimensions to help humanity. However, they hardly describe the dimensions as heaven, hell, Sheol, the world-to-come, or purgatory, but they knew of these dimensions before any organized religion came into being.

The Ifá priests know the language of plants and thus could communicate with them. Such communication usually is in the form of listening to the plants tell their efficacies. It is of no surprise to a priest to hear a plant tell its efficacy and style for its prescription. So, in the plant land, there are plants for all sorts of medication: some for good and some for not-so-good intents. Perhaps, you might be wondering that science has opined that only humans can speak. Well, now you know that plants have language too.

Medicine Wo/Man: *A medicine man or medicine woman is a traditional healer and spiritual leader who is engaged in the service of a community of indigenous people. Various communities may have a* *different name for a medicine man, but, in general, they essentially perform the same services as the shamans and Santeria priestesses. They are the go-between for nature and the supernatural in their respective indigenous communities. They are great chemists who get their knowledge of plant medicine from the other dimension. It is not unusual for medicine men, Ifá priests, and shamans to combine spiritual and plant medicine in their practices. They must learn and take directions from the other dimension. Medicine men are common in Africa and in the Americas with the Native Americans. Medicine men have always known that there are other worlds besides ours because they communicate with that other world at a whim.*

Chapter Eight   In My Father's House

John 14:2

This author is attracted to the Old Testament because the books therein are a narrative of history. History, we were taught, are stories of past events and those who made those events happen. This has always been why immersing all endeavor to understanding all of it becomes a lifelong learning journey.

In most of the works, quoting any book of Old Testament comes with ease because we can fathom the truth behind the quoted texts. In discussions with people of the cloth, they drew my attention to John 14, which they point to as a confirmation of a "Heaven."

They suggested a read and a reread of John 14. The Chapter had been read many times earlier. What was not disclosed to them was my doubts on the foundation on which the New Testament was written. Thoughts about this and other matters were expressed in the book ***The Greatest Celestial Deception***.

There are questions regarding personification and the historicized/historicism of the Star of the New Testament. This work was given to some of my proof readers. They all asked me to read John 14:2. It is the go-to verse for most religionists, especially Christians.

Perhaps, they want to remind us that Jesus, Himself, made a confirmation of the existence of a Heaven. In the New Testament, it is very interesting that Jesus Christ could speak.

Well, that Chapter John 14 was fun and interesting. There aren't many big problems in ancient writings—one of which is the Bible. The problems facing ancient writings lie in the interpretation or outright misinterpretation of the texts. The Bible suffers greatly because the authors intended meanings are out-rightly misrepresented. One other problem is that of allegories and how they are interpreted.

As an ancient writing, the Bible is known to notoriously employ the tool of allegories. From confusing for some, to comforting for others, that verse (John 14:2) will go to earn mixed reviews as to its exact meaning.

Isn't this an allegory? Or does Heaven have many mansions or rooms? Rooms or mansions, you think? What other allegory—the biggest allegory, can you find in the Bible?

In speaking to His disciples, Jesus spoke these words on John 14:1-3

1 Let not your heart be troubled: ye believe in God, believe also in me.

2 In my Father's house are many mansions*: if it were not so, I would have told you. I go to prepare a place for you.*

3 And if I go and prepare a place for you, I will come again, and receive you unto myself; that where I am, there ye may be also.

Are these words not unusual? They're highly, highly unusual. Perhaps, you can visualize in your mind's eye multilevel thousands or multi-million roomed mansions where the praises of a God are performed constantly. This description makes "Heaven" a tangible place. Or is it? Reminds us of the mansion in New York called the Empire State Building.

Perhaps, it was a metaphor. Even so, would His followers understand a metaphor for Heaven that implies that, within the dwelling place of God, are situated millions and millions of roomed "mansions"?

For believers in a destination/ dimension called Heaven, there wasn't the slightest acknowledgment that there might be any problem. And that complete blindness, that knee-jerk defensive reaction to any kind of criticism or doubt, and or push back to their interpretation of a heaven, I'm afraid, is what defines the believers in Heaven.

There is the need to sell beliefs/ideologies and draw converts following the longstanding tradition in the New Testament which encourages a convert to be fishers of men. With converts who are fishers of men, it makes any opposing argument a fair game for attack and would be ultimately dismissed.

But for readers of the Bible looking inside from outside, watching the religious teachings, woven between all the bombshells are a stark reminder of the immense power of the *big lies* once you are hooked.

With the *big lies* and with *time*, a level of negative impact can be measured. Such disinformation, misinformation etc., has helped erode the convert's logical reasoning abilities, and thus, mental health.

Before you make up your mind about John 14:2, you are invited to read *The Greatest Celestial Deception: About the Bright Morning Star.* Sometimes, when some things are too good to be good, it is time to do some serious research to get some understanding.

In The Greatest Celestial Deception, we take you on a profound journey into the heart of ancient mind-set and practices, revealing a breathtaking, hidden reality that will transform your life forever and in many ways.

Perhaps, this Chapter could make us, you and I, not be like a moon reflecting the light of which ever sun that shines on it. A euphemism for aligning oneself with fair weather or herd mentality.

That sun is the misinformation and the disinformation—the big lies—directed and shone on us, all, 24/7. Heaven, as a dimension/destination, has existed "cocooned in a bubble of deception for good or bad as a tool to instill fear to the feeble minds.

If you have doubts, read up on Isaiah 14:12-16. In those five verses, the Bible was summarized. You can see Satan and Jesus. Heaven & Hell.

Bible secrets were not revealed because the authors had nothing to hide. They wrote it as is. It is those who crave power and riches that orchestrates the disinformation, misinformation etc., so as to plant fear.

The Gods, too, had nothing to hide. They told mankind the truth, the whole truth and no alternate versions. But our teachers are bending the truth of the Bible and books like the Bible.

Chapter Nine   Is There a Heaven—the Reality

If yes— show the proof

We must reach an inflexion point here, somehow. Inflexion point is explained away as: those events that result in a significant change in the progress of a geopolitical situation that becomes a turning point after which there is a dramatic change, positive or negative, that is expected to result.

You will read some mind-blowing factual interpretations of the Bible that you have read all the days of your lives, yet, unable to understand, but decided to understand according to your preachers' interpretations.

Perhaps, all the preachers have their personal opinions and truths according to their experiences, but they do not have a monopoly to the real truth.

You have reached an inflection point. You will notice the truth and "big lies" for your selves. And you will decide.

Heaven, as a word, adjective, and a destination was used so many times in the Book. It is not as if Heaven is "News." But it seems Heaven is about to become "News" based on what you are about to read here.

Elijah was taken to Heaven, so, the words were interpreted to readers of the Bible. Did those events actually happen? Of course, the events did happen. The Bible calls it like it is. But people with agendas interpret the verses to suit those agendas.

How was Elijah taken to heaven? Please, pay special attention here. In the first verse, it was categorically stated that Elijah would be taken to Heaven. Below is the Bible's narrative in 2 Kings 2:1-11

1 And it came to pass, when the LORD would take up Elijah into heaven by a whirlwind, that Elijah went with Elisha from Gilgal.
2 And Elijah said unto Elisha, Tarry here, I pray thee; for the LORD hath sent me to Bethel. And Elisha said *unto him, As* the LORD liveth, and *as* thy soul liveth, I will not leave thee. So they went down to Bethel.

3 And the sons of the prophets that *were* at Bethel came forth to Elisha, and said unto him, Knowest thou that the LORD will take away thy master from thy head to day? And he said, Yea, I know *it*; hold ye your peace.
4 And Elijah said unto him, Elisha, tarry here, I pray thee; for the LORD hath sent me to Jericho. And he said, *As* the LORD liveth, and *as* thy soul liveth, I will not leave thee. So they came to Jericho.
5 And the sons of the prophets that *were* at Jericho came to Elisha, and said unto him, Knowest thou that the LORD will take away thy master from thy head to day? And he answered, Yea, I know *it*; hold ye your peace.
6 And Elijah said unto him, Tarry, I pray thee, here; for the LORD hath sent me to Jordan. And he said, *As* the LORD liveth, and *as* thy soul liveth, I will not leave thee. And they two went on.
7 And fifty men of the sons of the prophets went, and stood to view afar off: and they two stood by Jordan.
8 And Elijah took his mantle, and wrapped *it* together, and smote the waters, and they were divided hither and thither, so that they two went over on dry ground.
9 And it came to pass, when they were gone over, that Elijah said unto Elisha, Ask what I

shall do for thee, before I be taken away from thee. And Elisha said, I pray thee, let a double portion of thy spirit be upon me.
10 And he said, Thou hast asked a hard thing: *nevertheless*, if thou see me *when I am* taken from thee, it shall be so unto thee; but if not, it shall not be *so*.
11 And it came to pass, as they still went on, and talked, that, behold, *there appeared* a chariot of fire, and horses of fire, and parted them both asunder; and Elijah went up by a whirlwind into heaven.

Verse 11 mentions "Chariot of fire" & "Horses of fire" and whirlwind into Heaven. Can you put a finger on the event that just happened? Biological extraterrestrial entities have just executed an abduction of a human—Elijah.

Most Christians would interpret this event as Elijah being taken to Heaven. Well, was there a Heaven? Is this not a misinterpretation of *Heaven?*

If you have read *A Guide to Interpreting the Bible Correctly,* you already know that Heaven is another name for another kind of flying technology—the space monster mothership. It is in space. It is anchored in the heavens—space. It is a space vehicle and because they were called Heaven doesn't make them any more or less divine. So, Heaven exists in all reality.

You can now see that Heaven here is not a different dimension. This heaven is in our space interacting with humans. By the way, most Christians would claim that Elijah was one of a few individuals taken to Heaven without dying.

We say this because, subconsciously, we believe that Heaven is in another dimension—a dimension you can only reach after death. So, when we say that Elijah, among others, were taken to Heaven without death, we are misspeaking because that is not factually true.

Like Elijah was taken to mothership (spaceship), he was also returned to mother Earth after he received instructions. This event is simply an abduction—no more, no less. Preachers, believers, and congregants are, however, allowed to spin, interpret, and assimilate in a manner they deem acceptable. Perceptions, after all, is what your awareness makes of it.

There are other models of extraterrestrial flying technologies. Some of these models can replicate and shapeshift. They can also camouflage so that even if you are looking into the heavens and it is in your part of gaze, you will not see it. Their technologies are, indeed, out of this world. We, humans, are still scratching the surface when it comes to comparing our technologies with extraterrestrials.

Let's list a few more.

    a. The glory of the LORD.
    b. The LORD's glory.
    c. Spirit of the LORD—this premiered on Genesis 1:2. It appeared so early in biblical narratives. You may want to reread that verse again. Do not overlook the word *hovering*.
    d. The LORD's Spirit.
    e. The Cherubim
    f. Chariots of fire
    g. Horses of fire
    h. Living creatures
    i. Etc. & much more

Prophet Elijah was not the only one abducted in this manner. There were many instances of biblical abduction narratives.

Most often, the interpreters of these events salts and peppers the stories to suit their personal narratives and agendas.

Prophet Ezekiel's narratives about his own abduction was eye-opening. There he was minding his own business, and out of the heavens came roaring, these flying things, he saw with his own eyes.

And he so very well gave a fantastic description of what he had no idea of.

Most people versed in hermeneutics and even people of the cloth spin this event to make it look and sound spiritual and say it is a vision. Vision? What vision?

There was nothing spiritual, and it was no vision or a dream. It was simply an event—a physical one. This was Ezekiel's story taken from Chapter 1:3-5. You may wish to read the whole chapter, perhaps, the whole book of Ezekiel. I implore, you do so.

3 The word of the LORD came expressly unto Ezekiel the priest, the son of Buzi, in the land of the Chaldeans by the river Chebar; and the hand of the LORD was there upon him.

4 And I looked, and, behold, a whirlwind came out of the north, a great cloud, and a fire infolding itself, and a
brightness *was* about it, and out of the midst thereof as the colour of amber, out of the midst of the fire.
5 Also out of the midst thereof *came* the likeness of four living creatures. And this *was* their appearance; they had the likeness of a man.

Further in Chapter 3:12-14, Ezekiel narrates his abduction.

12 Then the spirit took me up, and I heard behind me a voice of a great rushing, *saying,* Blessed *be* the glory of the LORD from his place.
13 *I heard* also the noise of the wings of the living creatures that touched one another, and the noise of the wheels over against them, and a noise of a great rushing.
14 So the spirit lifted me up, and took me away, and I went in bitterness, in the heat of my spirit; but the hand of the LORD was strong upon me.

Look at these events and put them in perspective when compared with our technologies of today. We have the International Space Station (ISS). It is a modular space station. It is a habitable satellite in low Earth orbit.

This is one of mankind's greatest technological feats—putting men in orbit. Spaceships, bigger than cities exist and has been existing before Earth was seeded.

In fact, extraterrestrial satellites (sorry, Heaven) is bigger than the island of Hispaniola and Cuba combined. This is one of many extraterrestrial launching points to various galaxies in the Universe.

Space is not like land or planets. Space is almost limitless. If you have the technology, you can acquire as much of it as you desire.

To this end, don't be surprised if you read or understand from some sources that extraterrestrial satellites (Heaven) is bigger than many planets combined. They can also be floating megacities that are capable of replicating themselves.

Indeed, Gen 1:2 confirms this:

And the earth was without form, and void; and darkness *was* upon the face of the deep. And the Spirit of God moved upon the face of the waters.

The catchphrase here is: And the Spirit of God moved upon the face of the waters. Another version of KJV (not the online version) has this as: And the Spirit of God was hovering over the face of the waters.

Hovering is the descriptive give-away word here. A technology that could hover has existed before Earth was terraformed? So unbelievable, yet true. Mankind only recently developed technology that could hover. This is very believable and true.

That was at the time the planet Earth was discovered by the astronauts from "Heaven." The author(s) of this event were/was not hiding any "secrets" of Heaven. The narrative laid bare the truth.

Whether we understand it today, interpret it correctly, or spin it any way we deem fit is up to us. Most of us believe the spins and lies from the pulpit, but the Bible was true yesterday as it is today, and will be tomorrow. No spins can change the truth.

By Bible-speak, when astronauts are taken from Earth and flown into the spaceship, the huge flowing city like the mothership, it is akin to Heaven in the heavens.

So when the biological extraterrestrial entities kidnapped, sorry, abducted the "prophets" using the "spirits of the LORD" and taken to the huge mothership (spaceships), the event's narrator/writer/prophet assumed the spaceships as "Heaven." "Heaven," therefore, could be as large as a floating city/country/planet in space.

The sheer beauty of this technology called Heaven and the science it took to put her in space must be mind-blowing to a human who would not be able to fathom such technology. Do you then wonder that they nicknamed this technology—Heaven?

There were more encounters between biological man and biological extraterrestrial entities. There was the instance, where Moses—the Prophet—was requested to go to the mountain top. Let us let Exodus tell the story. Ex. 24:15-18

15 And Moses went up into the mount, and a cloud covered the mount.

16 And the glory of the LORD abode upon Mount Sinai, and the cloud covered it six days: and the seventh day he called unto Moses out of the midst of the cloud.
17 And the sight of the glory of the LORD *was* like devouring fire on the top of the mount in the eyes of the children of Israel.
18 And Moses went into the midst of the cloud, and gat him up into the mount: and Moses was in the mount forty days and forty nights.

Take note of the mention of the model space vehicle. The model of the flying space vehicle—the glory of the LORD. Thus, this is yet another example of the many encounters between the gods/angels and man. There were too many instances in the book of exodus to be recounted here.

But, there was yet another encounter with the sky space travelers that is too good to be true and left untold. It was so revealing about the space travelers that those who put the Bible together refused to add that book to the Bible. That book is the book of Enoch.

Enoch the prophet appeared quite early in Genesis. Enoch is the son of Jared, and the father of Methuselah. Gen 5:21-24 briefly narrated his chronology.

21 And Enoch lived sixty and five years, and begat Methuselah:

22 And Enoch walked with God after he begat Methuselah three hundred years, and begat sons and daughters:

23 And all the days of Enoch were three hundred sixty and five years:

24 And Enoch walked with God: and he *was* not; for God took him.

Look at verse 24. Its last phrase reads: for God took him. It ended abruptly, and so, some people assume that God took him to Heaven. He, therefore, was the other one of the two men taken to Heaven without death. The other being Prophet Elijah.

That is what some believe and preach. Yes, both men were taken to Heaven, but they were returned to mother Earth where they succumbed to the elements like every other living thing.

That is by the way.

Enoch interacted with "God" like no other. He walked with "God." He worked with "God." In another Abrahamic religion, Enoch was rumored to be the builder of the pyramids—the aligned Egyptian pyramids.

When the fallen angels fell into disfavor with "God," the angels asked Enoch to intercede on their behalf. Do not forget to remember that the so called fallen angels were the Children of God. He did intercede, but "God" would not change His mind.

Enoch learned the crafts of the sky visitors and chronicled the so called secrets of Heaven. He interacted in the very sense of interaction.

He even interacted with the extraterrestrial *big boss*. In fact, forget the Bible for a millionth seconds and concentrate on the book of Enoch, and you will get the mathematics, the biology, the physics, the technologies, the chemistry, cosmetics, the metallurgies of iron, the systems of agriculture etc. the subjects that were described as the "secrets of Heaven."

Enoch chronicled so much of these experiences and interactions, that the angels

who taught him these "secrets" were
accused of exposing the secrets of Heaven.

The Book of Enoch, which is also part of the
Jewish and Christian Apocrypha, gives
credence and credit to archangel Haniel who
had a travel plan to Earth on the assignment
from the Leader of the angels to abduct
Enoch in a (you guessed it) fiery chariot—a
description of a space vehicle—and fly
Enoch to a spaceship Enoch also called
Heaven.

Enoch, like other prophets then, called the
mighty city sized spaceship—a "Heaven."
Perhaps, *The Story of Archangel Haniel
Taking Enoch to Heaven* is best told by
Whitney Hopler, a religion expert.

And below, is a reproduction of part of the
story with minor modifications for clarity.

*The book of 3 Enoch features archangel Metatron
reflecting on what happened when archangel Haniel
came to take him on a trip from Earth to heaven. 3
Enoch 6:1-18 records:*

*"Rabbi Ishmael said: Metatron, the Angel, the Prince
of the Presence, said to me: 'When the Holy One,
blessed be He, desired to lift me up on high, He first
sent Anaphiel [another name for Haniel], the Prince,*

and he took me from their midst in their sight and carried me in great glory upon a fiery chariot with fiery horses, servants of glory. And He lifted me up to the high heavens, together with the Shekinah [the physical manifestation of God's glory].'"

'As soon as I reached the high heavens, the holy Chayot, the <u>Ophanim</u>, the Seraphim, the Cherubim, the wheels of the Merkaba (the Galgallim), and the ministers of the consuming fire, perceiving my smell from a distance of 365,000 myriads of parasangs, said: 'What smell of one born of a woman and what taste of a white drop is this that ascends on high? He is merely a gnat among those who divide flames of fire!'

The Holy One, blessed be He, answered and spoke to them: 'My servants, my hosts! Don't be displeased on account of this. Since all the children of men have denied me and my great kingdom and have gone worshiping idols, I have removed my Shekinah from among them and have lifted it up on high. But this one I have taken from among them is an elect one of the inhabitants of the world, and he is equal to all of them in faith, righteousness, and perfection of deed, and I have taken him as a tribute from my world under all the heavens.'"

It's interesting to note that the angels who encountered Enoch when he arrived in heaven detected the fact that he was a living human being by his scent and were upset about his presence there among the angels until God explained why he chose Enoch to come to heaven without dying first. In his book Tree of Souls: The Mythology of Judaism, *Howard Schwartz comments: "Enoch, like Noah, was a righteous man in his generation. He was the first among men who wrote down the signs of heaven. God saw the righteous ways of Enoch and called upon the angel Anafiel [another name for Haniel] to bring Enoch into heaven. An instant later Enoch found himself in a fiery chariot, drawn by fiery horses, ascending on high. As soon as the chariot reached heaven, the angels caught the scent of a living human and were ready to cast him out, for none among the living were permitted there. But God called out to the angels, saying, 'I have taken an elect one from among the inhabitants of Earth and have brought him here...'"*

Archangel Haniel's role as an angel who allows people into various heavenly places may be one of the reasons God chose Haniel to take Enoch into heaven. Not only is Haniel "a prince of angels who takes Enoch up to heaven in a fiery chariot in 3 Enoch," but Haniel "also holds the keys to the palaces of heaven,"

For the full article, there is reference in bibliography.

This important narrative especially about Prophet Enoch is that the Prophet was taken to "Heaven" in a flying space vehicle which our eyes can see. The Heaven that Enoch was taken to, also the eyes can see.

The residents of the Heaven Prophet Enoch was taken to have humanoid biological human ability's sense of smell. They weren't mechanical entities that can perform biological humanoid intellects.

Just as humans can sense the smell of a fish, the smell of a He-goat, and the smell of a dog, so did the biological extraterrestrials entities smell the scent of Enoch—a human, miles away before he was taken into "Heaven."

Perhaps, our human smell was so foul to the biological extraterrestrial aliens that their Leader—"God"—had to intervene by explaining the reason for Enoch's abduction and arrival onto "Heaven."

Perhaps, humans should be asking some questions, again, right about this time. Why were/are we being kidnapped? Have abductions stopped? Why were/are these space travelers interested in us? Why do they need space vehicles if "God" is omnipotent?

Perhaps, just one right answer to any of these questions would open our minds to wisdoms we usually do not have or have not thought about on our own, for a very long time or never.

Let's talk about the aliens' sense of smell a little bit more. It could be eye-opening. We, animals on earth, have some sense of smell, and we are also able to discern distinct animal and plant smells. It is biological. It is part of our intellects. Dogs have a tremendous sense of smell. That is biological.

Some people with a good sense of smell can detect the scent of a woman, the smell of a man and or the smell of a new born baby. In the jungle, some hunters can trace a specific animal through the power of smell. Some can smell a dangerous snake and take precautions where and when necessary. The ability to detect these variants in smell is biological.

The point being driven here is to draw your attention to the description and why the phrase—biological extraterrestrial entities— is used to describe "God & His angels." This is because they are also biological entities not mechanically and artificially controlled technology.

The sense of smell/odor has importance. This is because it is an experience. It is an awareness. If these extraterrestrials can smell us, perhaps, we can smell them too because according to Gen 1:26-27, God and His angels created man in His own image and likeness.

Here it is:
26 And God said, Let us make man in our image, after our likeness…
27 So God created man in his *own* image, in the image of God created he him; male and female created he them.

Prophet Enoch also told us about copulation between the extraterrestrials and earthly women. The prophet's story mimicked the Gen 6:4 narrative:

There were giants in the earth in those days; and also after that, when the sons of God came in unto the daughters of men, and they bare *children* to them, the same *became* mighty men which *were* of old, men of renown.

The takeaway from this story is the biological makeup of these extraterrestrials. There was/is a biological connection between humans and the extraterrestrial biological entities.

If they can make children with the earthly women, it must follow that the biological makeup of these so called angels is similar to that of Mankind.

Chapter Ten
Conclusion: Proof of Heaven

Common sense and truth have left the building long ago when you talk about the interpretations and misinterpretations of the authors' intended meanings in the books of the Bible.

Yes! There is a Heaven. In fact, there are many Heavens of different sizes. Heaven has fallen into the descriptions of a space station, a city, a ship, and or a floating station in space.

Heaven is not what you've been made to believe in and visualize in your mind's eyes. Heaven is a spaceship equipped with a laboratory, living quarters, launching stations for galactic space travels, storage facilities for the various flying machines and much more.

There was a question: how did you know that much about Heaven? Answer: the Bible told the stories. The Old Testament was/is very loud in its expressions and descriptions of Heaven. You need to learn the keys and keywords to decode the many allegories in the books.

Perhaps, a read of a few of my books will throw some light on the intentions of the writers of the books of the Old Testament.

It had been explained in details, sometimes, there is this feeling of repetition in the answers. If the repetitions would help to convince readers to the truth, then my purpose and intents have been met.

Heaven is a giant city in orbit/space. Heaven is one among many misunderstood technologies. To some people, Heaven is something, but to religionists, especially Christians and Christianity, Heaven is everything. This is why an understanding of what Heaven is, is profound.

Let us think for once. The Bible described what Heaven was/is. It was not a lie. The Old Testament was/is as usual very well on point with the truth. The Old Testament was/is precise on the details.

It was/is not the Bible's fault that some religionists chose to misconstrue the meaning of Heaven for reasons best known to them. There is a likelihood that this assertion will be repeated to show how important the point is.

Consciousness, as the All-Knowing Creator does not need a flying vehicle to visit the Earth and other planets and galaxies. Consciousness is actually omnipotent.

Somebody reminded me that they read books with proof of Heaven, and they too, in return, were reminded that the Bible is also a book about the proof of Heaven. You do not need to be in a state of near death experience (NDE) to see/understand the proof of Heaven. Heaven is practical. It is material. It is not immaterial. It may have the technologies for shapeshifting, replicating, vanishing, and reappearing (camouflage), yet, it is a construct—a place inhabited by biological extraterrestrial entities that look humanoid.

Heaven has always been under our noses, and you do not need to die to get there.

When man is technologically sufficient like the gods, we will be flying past the station called Heaven. Hopefully, someday, we will reach that level, but that will take thousands of years—even millions of years cannot be ruled out.

Some of us are stuck in reasonableness. We've become reasonable men. In years past, one of my law professors would always ask: What would a reasonable man do under this or that circumstance? What would a reasonable man think? Reasonableness has become like thinking within and not outside the box.

In effect, if science doesn't approve of it, it is irrelevant or it's called pseudo whatever. Science discovers what is existing—that which we do not know, yet. Science, too, is learning and having new experiences about our planet and this planetary system, other galactic systems and indeed the universe.

This reasonable man syndrome has its advantages, but it has its disadvantages, too. For one, it forces you to think like others as if there is only one way to be aware. It makes you see everything from a herd perspective.

Everybody must arrive at 4 by only 2 +2. But you can arrive @ 4 by also 1+3, 2*2 and 4*1. Therefore, while we can be reasonable, we can think outside the box to observe a different perspective. People have different awareness.

It does not mean that we must not always have things in perspective. The universe has been created or has metamorphosed. Everything it must be or not be has been programmed to evolve.

The universe is a program playing itself out. It has been set. There is no reprogramming. What will be has been set. What will be, will be. It has been set. Nothing can change the cause of the program. So, save it like it is and will ever be.

The lives that would show their faces on Earth and in other planets have been set in stone. All lives that will replenish the Earth have been set in the program. There is nothing anyone or anything can do about it.

The way this universe, like all other multiverses, would play out has been set.

Nothing happens that has not been programmed to happen. The Bible is telling us a beautiful story of superior science & technology, between primitive minds and biological extraterrestrial entities. What is happening, according to the programs which Consciousness has scripted, had been set in place.

Are we even able to understand these stories? Are we creating gods out of the stories witnessed by primitive minds with a lack of understanding of the superior technologies?

We are still confused by misunderstood technologies. We are confused by the constant use of certain terms in the biblical texts like allegories, zoomorphism, anthropomorphisms, etc. The style employed by writers of the books of the Old Testament makes it difficult to fathom the authors' intend meanings (AIM).

Anyhow you think of these biblical stories, keep this in mind. That this is a play by play description of Gods with superior and unfathomable technologies. It is the manifestation of "magical" technologies before a primitive mankind. The misunderstood technologies suddenly made god and angels out of the astronauts operating these technologies. And suddenly, words such as omnipotence and divineness started to take hold among the primitive minds of mankind.

How else could they have described what they do not understand? I loathe to write this, but for the purposes of explaining our forefathers' behaviors, did it even occur to you that even in this century, the Whiteman was described as next to the gods or from other planets in some societies/continents? This was so because where the natives had bows and arrows, the Whiteman had guns (albeit Dane-guns) and were quick to use it. The fear of those Dane-guns, as they say "was the beginning of wisdom."

That the ancient peoples interpreted the technologically advanced beings from the cosmos as God and His angels is fathomable and understandable. This is so because when superior science and technology meets primitive tools, the latter tends to worship the superior science and technologies.

They—the ancients—therefore, invented texts/adjectives/allegories to explain events they could not understand. The invented new texts/allegories were usually along the understanding of magic, and therefore, the taints of spirituality were introduced.

If you seriously and logically think about it, it was possible that this was exactly the same event that happened in the distant past, perhaps, many centuries ago.

Today, with the United States' technological power, especially in areas of war, it would be foolish, even suicidal, for a small country like Grenada, Cuba, Jamaica, or even the three of them combined to engage the United States in military warfare. Perhaps, our forefathers had that same fear of the gods. Did you see the word "perhaps"? Perhaps is not the word. Our forefathers were scared stiff. Not when Sodom and Gomorrah were being bombarded with nuclear weapons described as unquenchable fire and brimstone from

Heaven, it would be catastrophic not to be scared. It was hell on earth.

This curiosity of not knowing and that pattern of fear could have easily led to the deification and, therefore, the worship of the extraterrestrials—the people from the stars.

If anyone should logically draw a conclusion, that the curiosity and fear of what the gods might do, could lead a primitive mind to be overwhelmed by the superior technological achievements of a civilization from the heavens—that conclusion would be logically reasonable.

Perhaps, we have to draw a conclusion of whether there is a Heaven. To do that, we should likely draw a conclusion about Hell, too. For as we have constantly observed, using scripture to interpret scripture, if the scripture says, there is no Hell, there is no Heaven either—at least, not in the sense we have been taught to visualize that place called Heaven.

Perhaps, our interpretation of the biblical texts is suspect. Perhaps, Heaven is an allegory like many things in the Bible.

We just have to decode it correctly. Therefore, there have never been this yin and yang dualism of good and bad that has been created all along. Good, being Heaven, and bad, being Hell. But how can that be if our purpose on Earth had been predetermined according to Akashic Records, a book even the Bible refers to as Book of Life?

Some people of the cloth will be remembered for their fits of envy and catastrophic missteps in interpretations of the verses of the Bible and other books like the Bible.

Misinterpretations have become like a pandemic ravaging the readers of the "holy" books. It is as if they are forced to misrepresent the meaning of the verses so as to assuage the fears of the people. What is this fear? Is it the people's fear of death or is it the leaders' fear of insurrection? Whatever fear it was/is, the use of religion to assuage the fears of the people is too huge to be unnoticed.

The bottom line is that religious houses and people of the cloth have produced the greatest failure in elevating enlightenment (spirituality) through leadership. Interpreting correctly and disseminating the truth—the authors' intended meanings—must be the preachers' intentions at all times.

Whether what we are witnessing today was/is a strategy to contain human behavior or simply an ignorance on the preachers/teachers' part will not change the disinformation already imparted to human minds.

It was/is situations such as these that make one remember Thomas Sowell when he said:

"It is hard to imagine a more stupid or more dangerous way of making decisions than by putting those decisions in the hands of people who pay no price for being wrong."

In the final analysis, there is a Heaven if you believe that a mothership (spaceship) by various names like Heaven, the glory of the lord, etc. is "Heaven" we've been conditioned to assimilate as the place to spend eternity. Elijah was taken up to one of those "Heaven(s)" in the heavens (space).

If, however, your perception of a Heaven is a destination in another dimension where the soul goes to enjoy the eternity in an afterlife, the Old Testament did not say such a place existed or exists. If anything, the Old Testament makes it abundantly clear that there is not a hell just like there is no Heaven where eternity is spent.

By the way, when the Bible tells us that certain prophets were taken to Heaven, it must rekindle something in your mind. It should make you think: how is it possible that humans in flesh were taken to Heaven?

The Heaven we were made to understand is not accessible in flesh. Therefore, if humans were able to access Heaven as narrated in the Bible, then, just as humans are flesh, Heaven is physical. And thus far, you understand that to be true. Don't fall for the translations of the people of the cloth. They don't know any better. Most of them, if not all, are swimming in an ocean of ignorance.

If you argue that New Testament says otherwise, you're invited to first read *The Greatest Celestial Deception* before you draw a conclusion.

Don't lose hope, however, because the soul can neither be created nor destroyed. The souls are masters at recycling themselves by attaching to new bodies.

The new body the soul must possess had been decided already and is available for a reading if you so wish. It is available in the ethereal field known as the Akashic Records.

In fact, finding a *truth* should set us free as the saying goes. The questions that comes to mind could include: if there was no Heaven, then, who or what did Elijah, Moses, Ezekiel, Enoch interact with?

You see, there is a reason why there is a *biblical God* and **Consciousness** in my vocabulary when describing creations. One of those vocabularies describes biological extraterrestrial entities while the other describes the All-Knowing. By the way, there is no denying or spinning those interactions.

In fact, there are hundreds, if not thousands, of chronicled later interactions between the so called "fallen angels" and our earthly women.

The sexual interactions between earthly biological women and the biological extraterrestrial entities otherwise nicknamed fallen angels, gave us the biological giants known as Nephilim (Gen 6:4).

Such interactions/abductions are still taking place today. The hope is, that this work serves as a much needed and desired vaccine at the right time. If you know, you know.

Were the prophets' narratives true? When you understand the texts, the allegories, the context, etc., you know undeniably that the prophets were telling stories of what were seen, not some imagined stories. You start to piece together the stories in your head. You start to weave the stories in your head and all of sudden the events come alive.

Today, humans have a technology that can take us into deep space and the doors and windows of the space station would open up. The human walks through the door into the space station and stays for 40 days and 40 nights.

Then, another technology apparatus returns the human back to Earth where he would live out his remaining days before succumbing to the elements.

Now, how does the aforementioned scenario play in your imagination?

This is simply what Prophet Enoch and others were saying and explaining in their own words. These events were playing out thousands of years ago. Though, I have explained—in other writings of past civilizations (civilizations so superior to ours even to this day) our forefathers thought they were magical. They were indeed magical to the ancients because they did not understand the technologies.

Prophet Enoch, like many others, was kidnapped—abducted—by angels and whisked up into the heavens where the space station—Heaven—was anchored in space.

That Prophet Enoch called his abductors *angels* does not change that these were species from the heavens who were/are stationed in Motherships floating in space.

The motherships were/are space stations far, far away from where inter-galactic missions originate and are coordinated. That Prophet Enoch christened the Mothership a *Heaven* is understandable.

You were abducted into a mothership where there were bright lights, free food and water, nice sleeping space, free this and free that, and the technology that makes all these work is unbelievably described as divinely magical.

And this technological apparatus is high up in the heavens. There was/is no name more appropriate than *Heaven.* By the way, there are many Heaven(s). A constructive critic who read the manuscript for this work asked: how can you prove that there is more than one Heaven? The answer was so simple. If Heaven is a technological Mothership, if you can build one, you can build many.

If you remember that one of the technologies—flying space vehicles—was named "the glory of the LORD or the LORD's glory," then read Isaiah 6:1-3

1 In the year that King Uzziah died I saw also the Lord sitting upon a throne, high and lifted up, and his train filled the temple.
2 Above it stood the seraphims: each one had six wings; with twain he covered his face, and with twain he covered his feet, and with twain he did fly.
3 And one cried unto another, and said, Holy, holy, holy, is the LORD of hosts: the whole earth is full of his glory.

Take a special consideration of verse 3. *The whole earth is full of His glory* translates to: there are UFOs—unknown flying objects—all over the earth. And that does not exclude today.

You'd be surprised that the way it was yesterday is exactly the same way it is today. If there were UFOs today, our forefathers had already devised names for these space machines. Today, some of our supposedly reasonably "learned" people are still deliberately doubting the models of these space machines— "spirits of the LORDs," "the glory of the LORDs," "the seraphim"—and all the other models of spaceships, the Bible's Old Testament had been alluding to all along.

We need to have open minds so as to be able to relearn the many "secrets" that are in plain sight. Some secrets are even staring us in the face.

In one of my books—perhaps, more than one of my books—readers are reminded to learn to unlearn some, if not, most of what they have been made to learn, and start to relearn afresh. I was talking especially about religions, history, etc.

Today, we came across the writings of Alvin Toffler and one of his quotes delivered a perfect niche. It was very interesting.

He was quoted to have said that "The illiterate of the 21st century will not be those who cannot read and write, but those who cannot learn, unlearn, and relearn."

For the purposes of this work, those who can read the Bible texts are encouraged hereon to learn to unlearn the Bible and start afresh to relearn the Book. Soon, you will learn from the same Bible that:

Illustration: *Courtesy of iStockphoto. Imagine 1000 of these attached to one another in space.*

The Bible is the greatest historical record there is on Earth about extraterrestrials. The authors did not shy away from that.

Until you and I learn to read and interpret the Bible after we have learned and unlearned, we have to relearn the Bible again to understand that the Bible has a background with an understanding that angels are nothing more but extraterrestrials.

And that "Heaven is no more paramount like we have been "forced" to learn, understand, and believe.

There is no way, we will understand "those" people. They were/are humanoid looking extraterrestrials in space with technologies that could annihilate humans on planet Earth if they so wished and desired.

Angels are misinterpretations of aliens with flesh and blood from space. They could camouflage, shapeshift, and replicate. And that is because they have "magical" technologies we do not understand then and now.
These are characteristics that lend credence to an understanding that the angels are not

mere mythology or folklores but actual description of travelers from space—from the skies—that carried out kidnappings and abductions on behalf of their Leader.

Is it any wonder that our forefathers were so scared of them and thought of them as God (s)?

You see, modern day extraterrestrials are even smarter. Mankind is also smarter and that makes the angels to worry. Mankind is irrational. Angels understand their own history of irrationalities.

They do not want what had happened to them to happen to mankind. You may want to read my book *All the God We Cannot See*. The book makes it clear that angels are no different to mankind. The book was written to make stubborn realities manifest.

There are times when silence is equated to betrayal. Your mind must not be left to continue to wobble like the legs of a newborn horse. Extraterrestrials know that Ages are opening unknown knowledge to mankind. Mankind is rapidly advancing, and this is because the angels gave their permission. If we didn't have their permission, we cannot test-shoot a rocket into space. They will immediately dismantle it. This is not hearsay or make-believe. It is already happening.

Today, Mankind has built nuclear technology, and the angels do not like that, we have that technology. This is because they understand from their own angelic/extraterrestrial experiences. They know the impact a nuclear bomb can have on the environment. They know.

They very much know better than we do. If you already read some of my books, you, perhaps, already know that Sodom and Gomorrah were destroyed by nuclear technologies by the angels.

The gain of unlearning and relearning the books could have many advantages that could come in many folds.

One, you become aware. Two, you now know the true history and operations of space dwellers and their technologies. Three, you become free from the misinformation that some have come to label as big lies. Fourth, you may be shocked to learn that your savings account may suddenly get fat because teachings such as tithing becomes irrelevant.

This does not mean giving to charity is a waste that should be abandoned. In fact, now is the shocking moment to give because what you plant will be what your soul will reap, unless you want to be reincarnating to earth.

The soul is living through you. The soul is Consciousness experiencing this earth through you. The soul is the Almighty Creator. That, you already know if you'd followed my writings. These and more are the reasons you now must serve humanity because you now know that life is from One Source.

Finally, if you buy into my conclusion, you may want to tell your friends that this book can be read on many different levels. Firstly, it may be read by ordinary non-religious people with a limited, if any, religious background.

Throughout, the book has been written with the irreligious and religionists audience in mind. At times, the science presented might seem miniscule, but when you really come around to thinking about it, you begin to understand that the religion expressed in the Old Testament is indeed science and technology, explained away as religion. There is a realization that this book—like some of my other books—will create some worries to some readers.

If you have been my fan, you already know it has never been easy to challenge the controllers of the System – of any kind, in any context. The advocates of the status quo don't want to lose their status, so they will be on the onslaught by all means necessary.

Having spent years in the field of Bible Studies and having published over 12 books, it is because I feel obliged to share my knowledge, analyses, and conclusions.

Hopefully, my accounts will raise the level of awareness among religionists and the irreligious to initiate a different and truthful discussion that will, in turn, contribute to our studies of the extraterrestrial biological entities we collectively refer to as God and His angels.

The hope is that this book is widely read. If we are to avoid the blunders of the past, then we need to change the direction and start benefiting from the knowledge base created by the authors of the books of the Old Testament that explains away science and technology in religious terms.

The Ages are opening up the concealed knowledge base unknown to man, many years ago. We did not have this chance some decades ago. Now is the right time. The right time to know.

Good luck!

Hi there, we say thank you for buying and reading. If you've read thus far, a review of this work would be very much appreciated. Thank you in advance of a review.

Below are more books by Sam Oputa

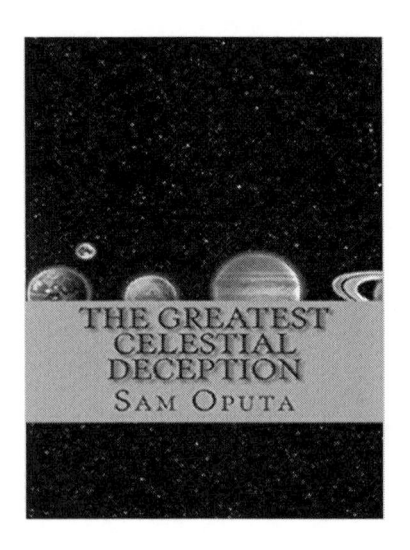

THE GREATEST CELESTIAL DECEPTION

SAM OPUTA

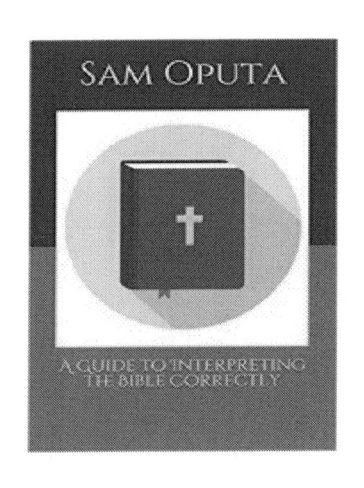

SAM OPUTA

A GUIDE TO INTERPRETING THE BIBLE CORRECTLY

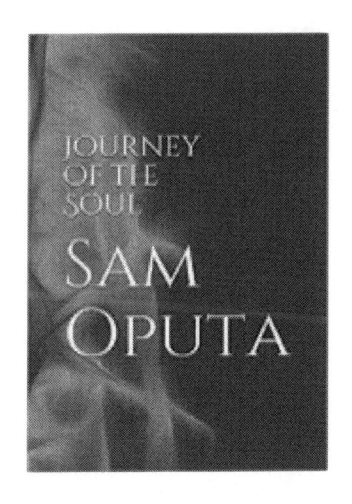

JOURNEY OF THE SOUL

SAM OPUTA

Akashic Records Or Free Will
Finding Your Calling

Sam Oputa

WHY WAS MAN CREATED?

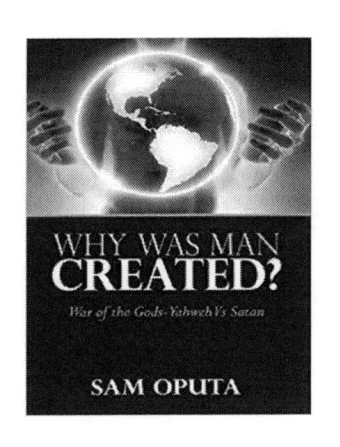

War of the Gods-Yahweh Vs Satan

SAM OPUTA

IMMATERIAL EXISTENCE
Sam Oputa

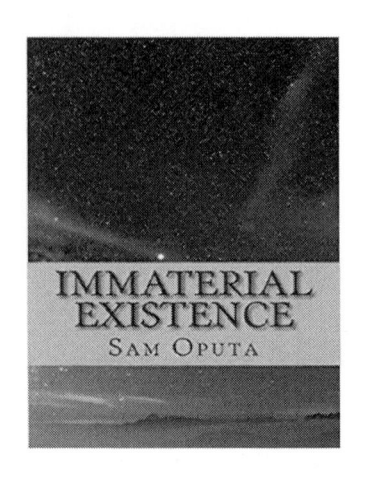

Bibliography

All Bible Quotes are from
https://www.kingjamesbibleonline.org/
unless otherwise stated.

Hopler, Whitney. (2021, February 8). The Story of Archangel Haniel Taking Enoch to Heaven. Retrieved from
https://www.learnreligions.com/archangel-haniel-enoch-124046

Janis, I. (1972 Victims of Groupthink.).

Retrieved from
https://www.jstor.org/stable/3791464?seq=1

Manufactured by Amazon.ca
Bolton, ON